FROM DIVERSITY TO INCLUSION: THE POWER OF LEADERSHIP & TEAM BUILDING

3 PROVEN STRATEGIES FOR LEADERS TO CREATE UNBREAKABLE TEAMS WHILE NAVIGATING WORKPLACE DIVERSITY, EQUITY, AND INCLUSION CHALLENGES

JOHN MCCANN & KATIE MCCANN

THANK YOU!

We are THRILLED that you've chosen to embark on this fantastic leadership journey with us, and you're certainly in for a treat!

Now, here's a little gift to make your leadership experience even more incredible – a FREE Leadership Workbook to supercharge your skills!

Scan this QR Code for your digital workbook, **Leading with Confidence**!

If you're more of a clicker than a scanner, no worries! Simply visit this link to get your hands on the free workbook by going to: https://katiemccann11.systeme. io/unlockyourleadership

Join our Facebook Community!

Being a leader doesn't mean you have to go it alone! Join our Lead & Succeed Facebook Community where we share tips, tricks, and hilarious leadership stories!

Thanks for embarking on this adventure with us! Together, we'll unlock the superhero leader within you!

All our best,

John & Katie McCann

Your Privacy is Our Priority: Your trust means everything to us, and we promise not to break it. By sharing your email address and getting the free workbook, you're giving us a virtual fist bump, and we'll keep you in the loop with occasional leadership nuggets. Don't worry; we won't share your info with anyone else! You can part ways anytime with a simple click!

TABLE OF CONTENTS

INTRODUCTION

People will typically be more enthusiastic where they feel a sense of belonging and see themselves as part of a community than they will in a workplace in which each person is left to his own devices. –Alfie Kohn

Did you know that a third of your life will be spent at work? That adds up to 9,000 days and 72,000 hours at the office. Your level of satisfaction at work matters because it can determine the quality of your overall well-being.

Many employees are waking up to the realization that their job satisfaction isn't predicted by salary increases and bonuses alone. It is also impacted by the sense of belonging they feel at work. According to Maslow's Hierarchy of Needs, a sense of belonging falls on the third level. Human beings not only need food and water to survive but to feel like they belong in a community.

While the workplace isn't necessarily a place where you go to make friends, the general attitude and mindset you have toward work and fellow coworkers can cultivate a sense of belonging. There is nothing worse than having the "Sunday Blues," where you start feeling anxious just thinking about stepping into a work environment that doesn't value nor accommodate your needs as an employee.

Before we go any further, we must define what exactly we are speaking about when mentioning diversity, equity, and inclusion (DEI). First and foremost, DEI is a term used to describe programs and policies that seek to promote the participation and representation of minority and marginalized social groups at work. These groups may be categorized by age, gender, race, ethnicity, religion, disability, culture, and sexual orientation.

As separate terms, diversity refers to differences in people, ranging from their cultures to their work styles and personalities. Elements of diversity include demographics, educational background, socio-economic status, marital status, physical abilities, and mental abilities. Diverse teams are those that embrace differences amongst team members rather than advocating for uniformity in identity and expression.

Equity is often confused with equality, although they refer to different concepts. Equality means treating every employee the same and offering them the same amount of resources and opportunities. On the surface, this is what every organization wants—to treat employees equally. However, diverse teams consist of employees who did not receive the same start in life and therefore enter the workplace already at a loss.

For example, even though men and women have the right to work, women enter the workforce at a disadvantage due to balancing caregiving at home and still putting in the hours to advance their careers. This heavy load on their shoulders has a ripple effect when it comes to their career and financial advancement. Equity goes beyond equality and seeks to recognize each employee's background, which impacts their performance and development at work, then award resources and opportunities according to their unique circumstances.

Then we have the third concept of inclusion, which refers to making sure that every employee feels accepted at work. This concept is closely tied to the sense of belonging that we all desire to feel when placed in a group setting. Inclusive teams are those that create and reinforce a culture of open communication, collaboration, and participation. Essentially, by improving diversity and equity, teams are able to become more inclusive and establish a positive and supportive work environment.

The best way to understand who is represented by DEI programs and policies is to consider minority and marginalized groups in society; the same social dynamics and hierarchies are often reinforced at work, which is why there are efforts to correct these inequalities.

For instance, statistics show that in 2020, women earned 80 cents for every dollar earned by men; and women only occupied 26% of leadership roles (Gitnux, 2023). More recent statistics published in 2023 show that ethnic minorities (i.e., marginalized ethnic groups such as the Hispanic, Asian, African American, American Indian, and Alaska Native) make up 10% of the entire workforce and 6% of senior management positions. Moreover, 24% of Hispanic and African American employees report experiencing discrimination at work, compared to 15% of Caucasian employees (Gitnux, 2023a).

Diversity, equity, and inclusion are hot topics in the corporate world right now. U.S. companies have gone as far as creating specific departments that respond to these core values of human relations and spend over $8 billion a year on programs and training initiatives to support teams in adopting these values (Williams & Dolkas, 2022). Yet despite investing so much into these initiatives, data shows that not much has changed. In fact, one research study showed that the positive results of some DEI programs only last for about two days.

There are plenty of reasons why some DEI programs don't work. The first is the unrealistic expectations placed on employees to change after attending a once-off training workshop or weekend team-building. Another reason is implementing DEI programs without adjusting workplace policies and systems. While the programs are good, the fundamental structures of the organizations don't support positive change. Research conducted by Deloitte also showed that DEI programs were more likely to be sustainable and help to achieve business outcomes when coupled with inclusive leadership (Hawley, 2023).

To avoid spending hundreds of thousands, if not millions of dollars, on DEI policies and programs that look good on paper but have no real impact, it is important to take a moment and learn how diverse, equitable, and inclusive teams and cultures are built. The purpose of this book is to offer you insight into how to do just that!

Authors John and Katie McCann both have leadership experience with large and small companies and now work together as leaders in their family business. Together, they bring a wealth of experience in building and managing successful teams with mutual trust and respect. After reading this book, you too will understand what it takes to be a great leader and maintain a positive team culture which will help you achieve your personal and organizational goals.

From Diversity to Inclusion: The Power of Leadership & Team Building is written for professionals who care about their workplace and desire to bring about meaningful change. You may be in a leadership position or perhaps want to present information to your leader on how your team can adopt DEI practices that represent the interests of all employees. You will get to learn more about the diversity, equity, and inclusion challenges encountered in the workplace and discover the three C's of effective team building: communicate, collaborate, and create—as well as how to implement them in your team.

By implementing the three C's outlined in the book, you will gain the confidence and knowledge to create a culture of diversity, inclusion, and equity that will not only benefit the company and its stakeholders but also create a positive impact on society!

PART I

UNDERSTANDING BIAS AND DISCRIMINATION IN THE WORKPLACE

DIVERSITY, EQUITY, AND INCLUSION CHALLENGES IN THE WORKPLACE

Equality is leaving the door open for anyone who has the means to approach it; equity is ensuring there is a pathway to that door for those who need it.

— CAROLINE BELDEN

WHAT DIVERSITY, EQUITY, AND INCLUSION IS NOT

Even though DEI forms the basis of employee relations, many companies don't quite understand what it is and why it is so important. The sad reality is that the "norm" in most work-places is a culture of exclusion. Stepping into the work environment, marginalized groups of employees feel unwelcome as they are. To get along with the privileged group (usually a small group of Caucasian male or female employees), they are forced to assimilate into their culture and adopt their standards to get ahead.

Major companies like Amazon and Google have had charges leveled against them due to a lack of workplace inclusion. Marginalized ex-employees have filed lawsuits over alleged pay inequality, racial discrimination, microaggressions, and lack of representation in senior leadership roles (Srinivasan, 2021).

It may seem odd that big tech companies that are leaders in innovation still seem to get DEI wrong, but the truth is that, like many other organizations, they are misinformed when it comes to implementing DEI. It takes more than a large recruitment budget spent on hiring marginalized groups to take the problem of a lack of inclusivity away. The mistake that a lot of companies make is to focus on diversity without creating strategies for inclusivity.

Of course, diversity is a great place to start when seeking to create equal opportunities for work. It is important to consciously build teams that consist of people from different socio-economic backgrounds. However, diversity efforts tend to fail in work environments that lack inclusivity. While you are able to get different types of employees through the company doors, they may not feel welcome.

A 2021 diversity report released by Google highlighted the efforts the company had been making to promote diversity. The report began by mentioning all of the many DEI initiatives the company had implemented, such as spending $55 million to increase economic empowerment for women and taking 84% of their managers through unconscious bias training (Johansson, 2021). Yet despite their efforts, the report also revealed that ethnic minorities were not staying very long at the company.

For example, hiring for African American employees increased from 5.5% to 8.8% between 2020 and 2021. However, the attrition index (Google's measure of how many staff are leaving the company) showed an increase in Black staff turnover within the same period (2020–2021). Within a space of a year, the attrition index showed a jump from 112 to 121 of resigning African American employees (higher attrition rates were reported in African American female employees) (Johansson, 2021).

The reality is that giving marginalized groups access into an organization is only the first step to DEI and cannot be treated as the last. Feeling like an outsider when you are already working at a company hurts a lot more than being barred from entering. DEI is not about celebrating a higher number of women or people of color in office positions but rather making sure these minority groups feel accepted and supported by the company culture.

BARRIERS TO DIVERSITY AND REPRESENTATION IN THE WORKPLACE

When investigating the challenges associated with DEI in the workplace, it is important to consider a range of issues that can negatively impact the work culture. Part of your strategy to make your organization more diverse, equitable, and inclusive must involve responding to these issues with effective solutions. Below are some of the common challenges impacting diversity and representation efforts at work:

- **Lack of buy-in from the top.** Without the buy-in of managers and senior leaders in a company, DEI efforts are unsustainable. Indeed, they might create the policies, but what does that mean if nobody is actively enforcing them or holding decision-makers accountable?

Furthermore, not every employee will be excited about implementing these changes; some who aren't personally affected by the lack of inclusivity may even resist the change. Therefore, managers cannot step back and wait for employees to take the lead in these efforts because it may lead to team conflict and factionalism.

- **Different perspectives and expectations.** DEI may be an important criterion for satisfaction at work for marginalized employees, but the reality is that marginalized employees are the minority. There are comparatively more employees who are satisfied with the status quo and are unaware of how it may be discriminatory to others.

Managers and leaders who don't see the value in DEI may be hesitant to implement such initiatives. They may fear that being more diverse and inclusive might change the work culture for the worse. Until everybody on the team is on board and understands the necessity of DEI and how it can increase staff morale and productivity, they may continue to experience challenges in adopting these practices.

- **Lack of ongoing feedback.** Whenever any kind of change is implemented within an organization, ongoing feedback is essential. This is because decision-makers need to gain insight into how the new policies or practices affect workers. The lack of ongoing feedback makes it difficult to identify blind spots and adjust policies and practices accordingly.

Plus, decision-makers aren't able to gauge how well they are understanding and responding to employee grievances. Getting employees to provide ongoing feedback can be difficult if they lack trust in the leadership or fear being punished for speaking out about office problems. To help them feel safe giving feedback, employees should have access to many anonymous channels for sharing their thoughts and feelings.

- **Lack of goals and metrics.** While it is good to set up DEI initiatives, the planning stage is vital for success. Many organizations execute DEI programs without being clear on what they want to achieve and how they plan on measuring success.

There are also some organizations that come up with elaborate DEI objectives that look good on paper but aren't aligned with the organization's mission or values. While setting goals and proper key performance indicators (KPIs) takes more work, it allows organizations to identify the real issues affecting employees and keep track of progress over time.

- **Inadequate training.** Training is often how DEI programs are introduced to employees. Companies spend millions of dollars setting up workshops throughout the year to address diversity and inclusivity challenges at work. However, once these workshops are complete, employees go back to the office and continue as normal without carrying out those changes.

The reason for this is a lack of planning around how the principles taught will be implemented in the work environment. In other words, employees are taught skills that they aren't sure how to use in the real world. Once again, this is a planning issue that occurs due to a lack of sustainable actions being developed and taught.

The easiest part of developing DEI initiatives is the ideation phase. However, once you have come up with great ideas for promoting diversity and inclusion, there are a few challenges you will need to overcome. For instance, you will first need to get buy-in from managers and leaders who can model new changes and hold staff accountable to the updated work practices. But on the other hand, you must also ensure that employees are educated on the importance of DEI, that they are given the platform to voice their concerns and offer feedback, and that they are clear on how to relate to one another long after the training workshops are complete.

THE IMPACT OF UNCONSCIOUS BIAS AND DISCRIMINATION ON EMPLOYEES AND ORGANIZATIONS

Issues related to DEI in the workplace can be traced back to unconscious bias. We can define unconscious bias as a stereotype made toward a specific social group that is spread through social conditioning, media representations, and personal experiences. The problem with unconscious bias is that it exists on a subconscious level, which means that you are not always aware that you are relating to others based on ingrained stereotypes.

It isn't possible to just get rid of unconscious bias. After all, they provide a mental shortcut to help your brain quickly process and interpret information from the environment. For example, whenever you come across a person of color at work, there may be a range of thoughts and even emotions that your brain brings up to guide you through the interaction. If these thoughts or emotions are based on stereotypes that paint the person in a bad light, then you might intentionally or unintentionally commit microaggressions (verbal or non-verbal expressions of negative attitudes).

The first step in combating unconscious bias in the workplace is recognizing the different ways it can manifest. Below are examples of the different kinds of unconscious bias found in the workplace:

- **Racial bias.** Racial bias is a type of unconscious bias that assumes members of different races inherit distinct characteristics, which result in some races being superior to others. Members of superior racial groups receive privileges at work based on their race instead of merit. This type of attitude can perpetuate racism, where marginalized races are discriminated against in the office.
- **Gender bias.** Gender bias refers to the favoritism of one gender over another. Once again, this is often justified based on distinct characteristics that the superior gender possesses, which make them seem more reliable and competent at work than marginalized genders. This type of attitude can lead to discrimination based on gender, like women

being paid less per hour than men who perform similar job roles.

- **Affinity bias.** Affinity bias occurs when managers show a preference to employees who share similar interests, backgrounds, and personality traits as them. There may be a noticeable difference in how these employees are treated compared to other employees who may have different or opposite interests, backgrounds, and personality traits. For example, when opportunities for promotion arise, managers may select candidates based on their affinity toward them rather than skills.

- **Name bias.** Name bias occurs during the recruitment process, where certain names are favored over others. In most cases, names that are typically associated with English-speaking countries are preferred over names that are associated with foreign countries.

A report conducted by Raconteur found that job seekers from ethnic minority groups and white job seekers with non-English names had to send 60% more job applications to receive a favorable response from an employer than white job seekers with English names. When broken down by ethnic group, Pakistani job seekers had to send 70% more applications, followed by

Nigerian (80%) and North African or Middle Eastern (90%) (Crookes, 2021).

- **Age bias.** Age bias is a form of discrimination based on an employee's age. Certain stereotypes are made that either work in favor or against a young, middle-aged, or senior employee. For example, a senior employee may be perceived as non-progressive and resistant to technology, whereas a young employee may be seen as unreliable and lazy. This type of thinking can negatively impact employees' career development by making it hard for managers to take them seriously.

A major consequence of unconscious bias is that many qualified marginalized job seekers are unable to make it through the hiring process. However, even after they have been hired, they may feel alienated or discriminated against due to work policies, remuneration structures, or team cultures that reinforce unconscious bias. The presence of unconscious bias can negatively impact teams within the organization and cause office politics.

It is important to address unconscious bias by first understanding your own biases that you may be carrying. Harvard University researchers have created a free bias assessment tool that helps you measure your biases based on various categories. You can take the test by following this link: implicit.harvard.edu/implicit/takeatest.html. Take the time to reflect and confront your biases and how they might affect the people you work with.

WHY DIVERSITY AND REPRESENTATION MATTER

There are some companies that understand what DEI involves but are still apprehensive about embracing it. One of the reasons for this is a fear of offending employees. A poll created by Right Track Learning found that five out of ten workers are afraid of bringing up the topic of DEI in case they say the wrong thing (Cooney, 2021). These fears are somewhat justified since there has been an increase in people being threatened or publicly called out for saying or doing inappropriate things.

However, the rewards of starting these conversations at work and collaborating on ideas to improve diversity and representation among teams are far greater. DEI is a trend that is here to stay because more workers are being selective about where they work. To remain competitive and continue to produce quality work, organizations must summon the courage to confront barriers to DEI and improve the culture and spirit at work.

Below are a few reasons why it is important to start having open discussions around diversity and representation:

- **Support innovative thinking within teams.** One of the benefits of building diverse teams is the different kinds of perspectives employees can add when making decisions or solving problems. The diversity within a team encourages thinking outside the box, borrowing ideas from multiple fields and disciplines rather than sourcing ideas from the same pool of data all the time.
- **Attract and keep the best talent.** Word tends to spread very quickly about the type of work culture that exists in your office. Job seekers who care about diversity and inclusion will factor the quality of the workplace before making the decision to join or settle into your company.

A survey by Deloitte found that 59% of workers (and 67% of millennials) would prefer working at a company that advocates for gender equality and racial diversity (Ideas Fest, 2023). Feeling accepted as part of an organization can boost morale and encourage employees to participate in workplace activities and opportunities.

- **Achieve greater company goals.** When employees feel seen and valued, they are more likely to stay engaged with their work long enough to achieve company goals. Since their work environment feels supportive, they can maintain high performance and demonstrate loyalty toward your company's values and mission. The result is a win-win situation, where the business is growing, and employees feel fulfilled with their work.
- **Helps to understand a diverse customer base.** If your business caters to the needs of a diverse target market, then having a diverse team can improve your understanding and approach to selling and marketing to them. By collaborating with coworkers who represent subgroups of society, employees are able to identify specific pain points, needs, and ways to support different types of customers. Moreover, when customers see themselves in your business, they are more likely to choose you over competitors who may not represent their interests.
- **Encourage compassion across the organization.** When DEI efforts are

implemented throughout the organization, at every level and structure, it can transform how people treat each other within the company. The divisions among workers are replaced with a community culture that prioritizes the well-being of all employees above business profits. Everybody, at all levels, feels valued regardless of their job title. They are also able to trust that the leaders have their best interests at heart and seek more than anything to help them succeed in accomplishing their career goals.

TEAM BUILDING EXERCISE

Create a communication channel or group where employees can share photos of memories, special occasions, or funny moments that occur in their personal lives. When uploading a photo, ask them to describe the significance of that moment.

You can make the activity more engaging by having themes each week or month (i.e., family, anniversaries, childhood, school days, favorite meals, hobbies, etc). Make sure that you include rules on sharing and commenting on photos, such as prohibiting violent or inappropriate photos or negative, sarcastic comments.

IN SUMMARY

Undertaking DEI initiatives can be uncomfortable due to the type of conversations that need to be had, which require employees to step outside of their comfort zones. However, prioritizing DEI is the best way to attract and retain the best talent and invest in the growth of your company.

THE CAUSES OF A DYSFUNCTIONAL TEAM

If you do not lead by example, you cannot expect your team to follow.

— SRI AMIT RAY

THE ROLE OF TEAM LEADERS IN CREATING AN INCLUSIVE TEAM CULTURE

The responsibility for ensuring diversity and representation across an organization is often placed on managers when in fact, it is the responsibility of leaders to become advocates and role models for the type of inclusive workplace they envision.

For example, the hiring manager can follow a brief to hire X amount of Hispanic female employees to join the company. But if the people at the top are disengaged from the DEI recruitment initiative, they are not able to enforce the type of work environment that makes these workers feel welcome.

Therefore, everybody needs to be involved when seeking to improve diversity and representation, particularly leaders. Employees cannot rely on each other to create safe spaces; they need the support of leaders who can revise policies, introduce new practices, and provide channels for voicing concerns and sharing feedback.

Another important function of a leader is to build relationships with employees. This function alone can make workers from different backgrounds feel valued by their bosses. The ability to have open communication with executive members of the company sends a message to employees that it is acceptable to be themselves. Small gestures to build relationships with employees include asking about their pronouns, how to pronounce their names, and showing curiosity about their cultural or educational backgrounds.

There are four practical ways that leaders can actively work toward a more inclusive workplace, one where employees feel comfortable being themselves. These include:

- **Collect feedback.** An ongoing activity that leaders can perform is asking employees for feedback. The type of feedback gathered can revolve around different aspects of work life, ranging from task expectations to work culture. The purpose of collecting feedback is to provide ample opportunities for employees to feel heard. Nonetheless, this only becomes impactful when you respond to the feedback by taking action.
- **Encourage employees to step forward.** Employees who feel a sense of belonging at work are more likely to share feedback about their experiences. Thus, it is important to pay attention to the type of work environment you are creating with your decisions and behaviors.

Work environments that encourage employees to step forward and be a part of the change tend to create a positive and inclusive culture. Employees are empowered to speak up, even when they disagree with the direction the company is heading. They trust that even when they have different perspectives, their opinions are treated with respect.

- **Foster connections between employees.** Another responsibility that is assigned to leaders is to develop positive relationships among teams. Since leaders may not always be present during the planning and execution of projects, they must ensure that employees are comfortable working with each other and have the necessary skills to resolve problems and conflicts when they arise.

Furthermore, how employees feel working together is a strong predictor of job satisfaction and productivity. Leaders should create social networking opportunities and team-building events to encourage employees to get to know each other and form their own bonds, separate from the bonds they share with the leadership.

- **Recognize and reward employees.** Research shows that when employees are recognized on a weekly basis, they are twice as likely to say they feel included at work (Baumgartner, 2022). The caveat is that recognition must feel honest, authentic, and specific to the employee.

Recognizing diverse employees for various contributions to the organization ensures everybody knows that they matter to the success of the company. To promote inclusivity, it is important to recognize not only high achievement but also dedication, helpfulness, open-mindedness, taking initiative, and other desired qualities and values that promote the type of community-like work culture you want, where everyone feels welcome and appreciated.

THE CAUSES OF A DYSFUNCTIONAL TEAM

Author Patrick M. Lencioni wrote a book titled, *The Five Dysfunctions of a Team*, where he explored different kinds of team dynamics and offered strategies on how to improve team management (Lencioni, 2002).

Inside the book, Lencioni outlined five factors that threaten cohesion, open communication, and collaboration within teams. These factors are interrelated, meaning one factor can snowball and trigger another. In the end, this leads to a dysfunctional team that cannot work effectively together.

Below is a breakdown of the five factors mentioned in the book. As you go through each factor, consider how they might impact the level of inclusivity within your team.

Absence of Trust

Trust is an essential component of any relationship, including work relationships among employees. In the context of the work environment, trust can be defined as the level of confidence team members place in each other, which allows them to lower their defenses and have faith that their colleagues have their best interests at heart.

The absence of trust creates a negative ripple effect within teams, where employees are suspicious of each other and relate more like competitors than collaborators. This can create a tense environment that promotes dishonesty, gossip, backbiting behavior, concealing mistakes, passing blame, and forming smaller factions within teams.

Fear of Conflict

It is normal for coworkers to disagree on how to approach problems, which tasks to prioritize, when to set deadlines, how much work to assign to each person, and so on. As much as you would think the absence of conflict is ideal, in reality it can signal a lack of trust between colleagues.

In order to argue constructively, both parties need to be open about their difference of opinions. However, when there is a lack of trust, it is difficult to get parties to speak openly about their points of view or concerns. This creates a fear or avoidance of conflict, where employees pretend to agree on the surface and hide their true feelings about what they think or feel.

The fear of conflict can also show up in teams or departments where some employees are afraid to speak up due to being part of the minority (e.g., the only female in a male-dominated team). They may fear being judged or sabotaging future opportunities for career advancement by challenging decisions that protect the interests of the majority.

What's important to note is that the fear of conflict creates an atmosphere where employees cannot be themselves, and as a result, their productivity and job satisfaction may decrease. The inability to raise issues that affect how they work creates a lot of stress and can, at times, cause employees to resign, even when they are paid well.

Lack of Commitment

When there is a lack of trust and fear of conflict, team performance will be negatively impacted. This is because being engaged at work is strongly linked with job satisfaction. When employees aren't happy with their work environment or dynamics with colleagues, they may show less enthusiasm about achieving team goals.

In most cases, managers start to take notice of the dysfunction within teams when it gets to this point. However, the problem is often more complex than simply a lack of engagement or low morale. They may not see the dysfunctional patterns that have already formed and taken shape in the team.

The worst part about a lack of commitment is that getting employees to share their thoughts and feelings once they have disengaged is extremely difficult. The common trend in some companies is to introduce DEI initiatives at this particular stage of dysfunction. Many of these initiatives aren't effective or sustainable in the long run because of the unresolved issues that are at the root of problematic team dynamics.

Avoidance of Accountability

When teams lack commitment to their work tasks, they tend to avoid taking accountability for the quality of the outcomes. For instance, they may not feel obliged to respond to system failures, calm angry customers, or troubleshoot when they come across unexpected challenges.

This type of attitude can significantly impact the success of the team or company. It can also discourage employees from adopting a growth mindset, where they are motivated to continue upskilling themselves and improving their overall productivity.

Inattention to Results

The four factors mentioned above can snowball and lead to the fifth, which is inattention to results. This occurs when team members prioritize their own goals rather than working on shared goals. For example, due to a lack of trust, employees may be less willing to share ideas and resources or solve problems together. Subsequently, they may avoid collaborating on goals and instead choose to work independently.

There are two major issues with this. First, teams can misuse company resources when they fail to communicate and collaborate on projects. It may even cost the company more time and money to complete projects when team members are divided and can't seem to direct their energy to the same goal.

The second issue is that the individual interests of team members become more important than the collective interests of the team. In this type of work environment, conflict and office politics may be common, which worsens feelings of distrust and non-committal to work tasks.

Experiencing any of these challenges can be detrimental to the unity and health of your team. The aim is to respond to signs of these dysfunctional team dynamics immediately so they do not multiply and become difficult to resolve.

TEAM BUILDING EXERCISE

Encourage employees to create employee resource groups (ERG), which are virtual channels where employees with similar interests or experiences can meet to exchange ideas, socialize, and get to know each other better. Since these groups are employee-led, allow them to come up with their own topics or discussions. You can increase participation in this activity by incentivizing attending at least two ERG meetings per month. If possible, you can also dedicate a percentage of your office budget to funding ERG events, talks, and activities.

IN SUMMARY

As a leader, your organization is looking to you to set the tone for the type of work environment you promote at work. If you consider diversity and inclusivity important team values, then it is necessary to keep a watchful eye on dysfunctional team dynamics. You must deliberately create and enforce norms that encourage employees to be themselves and feel like valued members of your community.

THE CONSEQUENCES OF INEQUALITY AT WORK

In the end, as any successful teacher will tell you, you can only teach the things that you are. If we practice racism then it is racism we teach.

— MAX LERNER

HOW SOCIAL INEQUALITIES MANIFEST AT WORK

The two-year surge of COVID-19 brought about devastating outcomes to people across the world, both the employed and unemployed. However, what became strikingly noticeable was the present inequalities at work, which may have gone unnoticed before.

For example, due to lockdowns and other strict social regulations, many businesses had to shut down or terminate the contracts of many employees. Those most affected by the layoffs were low-wage workers, who made up approximately 80% of job losses (Gould & Kassa, 2021). But upon closer inspection of these findings, researchers found that marginalized workers were disproportionately impacted by job cuts. In particular, the study found that Black women, Hispanic women, as well as both genders in the Asian American and Pacific Islander (AAPI) groups recorded significant job losses.

The reason why so many marginalized workers lost their jobs is due to inequalities at work, namely that privileged groups (those closest to European origin) are more likely to be found and promoted in high-earning jobs. It isn't so much that they are exempt from job loss, but due to their positions within companies, they enjoy greater job security.

A 2021 study published by the Economic Policy Institute found that white workers made up 61.4% of the total U.S. workforce in professional occupations; the remainder was divided into Hispanic workers (17.4%), Black workers (12.8%), and AAPI workers (7.4%). In managerial positions, the following distribution was observed: White managers (72.5%), Hispanic managers (10.8%), Black managers (8.9%), and AAPI managers (7.1%) (Economic Policy Institute, 2021). These representation inequalities at work cause marginalized workers to incur a higher risk of joblessness than other groups.

Another trend that COVID-19 lockdowns and regulations revealed was the high number of working mothers, who experienced a disproportionate amount of pressure to keep their jobs while also taking on more parenting and household responsibilities. Mothers with small children suffered significant job losses due to the lack of access to childcare.

A Stateline analysis found that mothers of young children (12 years and under) lost 2.2 million jobs between the period of February and August 2020, compared to fathers of young children who lost 870,000 jobs (Henderson, 2020). Working mothers were, therefore, three times more vulnerable to unemployment than working fathers; figures were even worse for the single, working mothers, part of marginalized groups.

Even though these statistics look at the inequalities brought on by COVID-19, these issues have existed in corporate America for many centuries, dating back as far as the Atlantic Slave Trade, where people of color (more especially women) were exploited and systematically barred from accessing skilled, high-earning jobs. The pandemic simply exposed the discriminatory workplace norms that many marginalized workers had always been subjected to.

Nevertheless, the workplace inequalities that occurred during the pandemic were able to start an ongoing dialogue about the lack of DEI in some organizations and what they could do to become more inclusive of marginalized workers. Leaders also got the opportunity to learn about concepts like unconscious bias and the various practices that exist in the corporate world that disadvantage certain workers. Below we will look at some of these discriminatory practices and the subsequent implications.

EXAMPLES OF DISCRIMINATORY PRACTICES AT WORK

Discrimination is prevalent in unequal and inequitable workplaces. Despite what the company values may promote, the fact remains that employees aren't treated with the same level of care and consideration. The worst part is that there are no legitimate processes put in place to protect affected employees from bullying, unequal pay, favoritism, microaggression, or harassment. These types of cases get swept under the rug and wrongdoers aren't held accountable.

We can define discrimination as being treated unfavorably due to personal attributes, like the color of your skin, having a foreign accent, being a woman, or being a religious person. The root of discrimination is unconscious bias. Without reinforcing stereotypes about certain groups of people, there wouldn't be such a thing as acceptable or unacceptable personal attributes in society and at work. People would be accepted for who they are, and awarded on merit rather than what they represent.

No employee dreams of finding themselves at the receiving end of discrimination because it carries severe consequences, such as being

- turned down at a job interview.
- dismissed or given unnecessary warnings.
- denied training and career development opportunities.
- excluded from social work groups and events.
- left out of meetings and having important work-related information withheld from you.
- paid less than your peers who have similar work experience and perform similar duties.
- overloaded with work and given unrealistic deadlines.
- subjected to abuse or passive-aggressive behaviors due to your personal attributes.

- treated unfairly by your peers when you raise concerns or set work boundaries.

So, how exactly do discriminatory practices play out at work? The answer varies depending on how normalized the mistreatment of certain employees has become. In workplaces where discrimination is frowned upon yet reinforced through subtle ways, it can be difficult to hold wrongdoers accountable.

Employees who speak out against discrimination can sometimes face further victimization when they attempt to share their experiences. Since the discrimination cannot be seen in plain sight, they could be labeled as "troublemakers" who are seeking to cause a rift in the team or ruin the reputation of the company. The fear of being further victimized is what often prevents mistreated employees from voicing their concerns. However, this only perpetuates the cycle of abuse and a lack of accountability.

Below are some examples of discriminatory practices that occur in the workplace. Read through each example and reflect on similar experiences you have witnessed or heard about in the past. The aim is to get you comfortable hearing stories of discrimination so you are able to respond proactively to such cases in your workplace, but most importantly, validate the experiences of employees who come forward with similar issues.

Race Discrimination

Race discrimination occurs when an employee is mistreated due to racial stereotypes based on skin color, ethnicity, or nationality.

Case study:

Vikash was a professional sales rep who had been in the industry for over 15 years. When he started working for a particular customer service agency, his sales rate declined each month. It looked to his department manager that Vikash simply wasn't performing as hard as other sales reps.

The truth was he was having a hard time fitting in with his team. Being the only person of color, born and bred in a different country, he didn't look, sound, or think the same as other team members. People would often make fun of his accent, speak in a condescending tone, or make inappropriate jokes about his culture. He felt deeply self-conscious and undermined at work, and this negatively affected his mental well-being.

Age Discrimination

Age discrimination occurs when an employee is treated unfavorably because of their age. Certain assumptions are made about their competence, performance, or readiness for opportunities because of being seen as too young or old.

Case study:

Camille worked as a marketing assistant at a tech company. She was 20 years old when she arrived at the company, but she quickly settled in and became a valuable member of her team. However, despite her hard work, Camille noticed that other coworkers were getting promoted and she wasn't.

After three years of being an assistant and feeling demoralized about her career prospects, she decided to call a meeting with her supervisor. At the meeting, she finally got to hear the reason why she was being passed up for promotions. Her supervisor expressed that while Camille was a top performer, she didn't feel that she was mature enough to step into a higher position.

Sex and Gender-Based Discrimination

Sex and gender-based discrimination occurs when an employee is treated unfavorably because of how they choose to express their gender identity or sexuality at work.

Case study:

Kim is a lesbian who has a manly look and prefers to wear suits to work. In previous workplaces, she was always a victim of bullying from colleagues who weren't accepting of her identity and sexuality. Recently, her manager called a meeting and asked her to start dressing "appropriately." He mentioned how her choice of outfits was confusing to other colleagues and customers and didn't represent the values of the business.

Pregnancy Discrimination

Pregnancy discrimination refers to the unfair treatment working women experience when they fall pregnant, take maternity leave, or suffer from medical conditions related to pregnancy.

Case study:

Teisha was one of the top performers at a law firm. She had single-handedly brought in twice the number of clients as other lawyers combined. Her boss sang her praises and even offered to help her get promoted. However, this favor was taken away the moment she announced that she was expecting.

With each passing month, Teisha noticed that her coworkers weren't as eager to discuss business with her or offer to assist with projects. Many of them avoided her because they assumed she would be unpleasant to be around. Her boss said that she didn't need to come to work for the majority of her pregnancy until "she got back to her normal self." When she brought up the topic of a promotion, he regretfully said, "I need someone who will keep up with the demands of this position."

Disability Discrimination

Disability discrimination occurs when an employee is mistreated because of their disability. This causes them to feel like a nuisance or less deserving of the opportunity to work than their abled peers.

Case study:

A few years ago, Michael was diagnosed with depression. His mental illness caused him to visit the doctor regularly and miss days of work. After a few months, he was fired from his job. This came as a surprise to him because his productivity hadn't dropped since being diagnosed with depression. However, his supervisor cited a different reason for letting him go, which was that he "wasn't reliable."

To him, depressed people were lazy, complacent, and would sooner or later bring the whole team down. The process of finding a new job wasn't easy because many recruiters were under the same impression too. They were afraid to hire him because of the potential inconveniences his mental health would cause to the team.

Religious discrimination

Religious discrimination occurs when an employee is rejected based on their religious beliefs or banned from observing special religious customs, such as dressing a particular way.

Case study:

Mohammed was a qualified electrician who completed his degree in Bahrain and came to the US to look for work. For three years, he applied for contract and full-time positions at several companies but was never successful. He started to question whether his immigrant status was the cause of being turned down. Perhaps companies were biased against foreigners?

After the 50th rejection email, he decided to follow up and ask the recruiter why they had refused to hire him, despite meeting all of the job specifications. The recruiter hesitated at first to give a direct answer but eventually said that their recruitment policies discourage them from hiring Muslims. According to the recruiter, their company found the prayer breaks observed by Muslims to be "disruptive" to the rest of the organization.

Retaliation Discrimination

Retaliation discrimination occurs when an employee is blackmailed or alienated from others due to reporting cases of discrimination at work. This form of workplace discrimination is common in organizations where there is a lack of open communication and speaking against the company or its leaders is punishable.

Case study:

After six months of working at a marketing agency, Tameka started to feel uncomfortable collaborating on advertising campaigns with her team. She noticed the implicit biases that they held toward people of color, which were racist and depicted them in a negative light. For example, when profiling Black customers, the team would often depict them as loud, materialistic, and promiscuous.

As the only person of color on her team, she felt a strong urge to speak up. She assumed that because the team lacked diversity, many of her team members were misinformed about Black culture as well as the needs and desires of people of color. Speaking up caused tension between her and the team leader, who outrightly refuted the claims made against the team.

A week later, she was given a written warning for making accusatory claims that weren't backed with evidence. As the months went by, Tameka noticed that her colleagues were not as open to her anymore. They had found out about her meeting with the team lead and were told to be cautious of her because she was a troublemaker.

LAWS THAT PROTECT AGAINST WORKPLACE DISCRIMINATION

When employees face discrimination of any kind, they can feel helpless. However, there are laws put in place to protect them in such cases. It is also important for leaders to learn about these laws so they are aware of the type of legal protection employees have when lawsuits are made.

Below are four federal laws that were established by the U.S. Equal Employment Opportunity Commission (EEOC) that protect employees against workplace discrimination (deBara, 2023):

1. **Title VII of the Civil Rights Act (1964)**
   According to Title VII of the Civil Rights Act of
   1964, it is illegal to discriminate against an
   employee based on skin color, ethnicity,
   nationality, genetic information, religion, or
   sexual orientation. Title VII was amended to
   include the Pregnancy Discrimination Act,
   which made it illegal to discriminate against an
   employee based on pregnancy, childbirth, or
   pregnancy-related medical conditions.

2. **Age Discrimination in Employment Act
   (1967)** According to the Age Discrimination in
   Employment Act (ADEA) of 1967, it is illegal to
   discriminate against a potential employee in the
   recruitment process or a current employee
   working at the company based on their age.

3. **Americans with Disabilities Act (1990)**
   According to the Americans with Disabilities
   Act (ADA) of 1990, it is illegal to discriminate
   against potential or current employees based on
   their disabilities. The Act also states that
   necessary provisions must be made for
   employees with disabilities to ensure they have
   access to the same opportunities as other
   employees at work.

4. **Equal Pay Act (1963)** According to the Equal
   Pay Act (EPA) of 1963, it is illegal to pay male

and female workers unequal wages for the same work. In other words, male employees are not allowed to be paid higher salaries in comparison to female employees who hold similar positions by virtue of being a stereotypically favored gender.

Many states have additional laws that protect workers against other types of discrimination, such as discrimination based on marital status, familial status, and gender identity and expression. It is important to read up on laws enforced by the state your company operates under to understand the full spectrum of legal protection employees have against this type of inequality.

TEAM BUILDING EXERCISE

Provide sheets of paper and colorful markers for the whole team. If you have a large team, divide them into smaller groups of 5–8 people. Ask each person on a team to draw a flower with a large center and petals equivalent to the number of people on their team. For example, someone on a team of six people will draw a flower with a large center and six petals.

Inside the large center, ask each team member to write down common attributes among the people on the team. Thereafter, get them to populate each petal with unique attributes that each team member possesses. Give them sufficient time to think about what makes them similar and unique. As a team, have a discussion about each drawing and the interesting qualities that were mentioned. You can also open the floor for team members to explain or clarify their unique attributes.

IN SUMMARY

It is sometimes difficult to prevent social inequalities from entering the work environment. Employees can bring along their unconscious biases to work and interact with team members based on the stereotypes or assumptions they have learned and practiced in their personal lives. It is up to leaders to educate themselves on the many forms of discrimination that occur in a work environment to prevent such incidents from happening.

PART II

THE 3 C'S FOR LEADERS TO CREATE UNBREAKABLE TEAMS WHILE NAVIGATING WORKPLACE DIVERSITY, EQUITY, AND INCLUSION CHALLENGES

ENCOURAGE OPEN COMMUNICATION

Communication leads to community, that is, to understanding, intimacy and mutual valuing.

— ROLLO REECE MAY

THE DANGERS OF MISUNDERSTANDINGS WITHIN TEAMS

Heinrich is originally from Germany and tends to be direct and assertive. Unfortunately, he is under the assumption that his Canadian coworkers are the same. For example, before submitting work, he would ask the supervisor for feedback on his presentation. The supervisor would reply with some variation of "It's okay" or "I guess it's fine." After months of these seemingly positive interactions, Heinrich was called in for a performance review. The supervisor mentioned how the quality of his work was subpar and he needed to show more dedication.

Heinrich was confused. Didn't the supervisor say that his work was okay? What was really taking place between them was a cultural misunderstanding. In Canadian culture, being polite and friendly are important social values taught from an early age. The supervisor wasn't comfortable giving constructive criticism of his work out of fear of coming across as rude. On the other hand, Heinrich couldn't read between the lines and tell that the use of mundane expressions like "okay" and "fine" meant the supervisor was actually unimpressed with his work.

Taquisha was a new recruit, joining a team consisting of mostly white people. On the first day, she introduced herself to her manager, Linda, who followed up by asking if she had an easier name. Taquisha was visibly offended by the question and interpreted it as a sign of racism. She felt put down and discriminated against because of being born an African American.

However, this, too, was a cultural misunderstanding. Linda was not trying to be spiteful by asking for an alternative name; she was trying to break the ice and strike conversation. In hindsight, she realized how such a question might be insensitive when posed to a person of color due to historically being given white names and made to feel inferior because of their traditional names.

Greg was a team leader at an engineering firm, which hired mostly men. At the beginning of last year, the firm brought in its first female engineer, who would be assigned to Greg's team. He was so excited to have her join the team but, unfortunately, felt unprepared to mentor her.

In the first six months, Greg gave the female recruit easy projects that weren't as complex or demanding as projects other male coworkers were getting. She quickly realized what was happening and asked to be given more challenging work. Greg laughed and said that she wouldn't be able to cope with the workload. The female recruit walked away feeling dismissed and discriminated against based on her gender. She had the same qualifications and working experience as the men on her team and could therefore manage difficult projects.

She decided to write a formal complaint to express her concerns. When Greg read the complaint, he felt really embarrassed. All of this time, he thought that giving the recruit easy projects was a way of helping her get comfortable on the team. He feared that by assigning demanding projects early on, she would get over-whelmed and consider leaving the firm. But these intentions were lost in translation and instead seen as being sexist.

The common theme amongst these stories is the lack of open communication, which causes messages to get misconstrued and interpreted as something else. In diverse teams, the lack of open communication leads to frequent misunderstandings about the intent of what is being spoken. Since team members come from different social and cultural backgrounds, they often interpret messages through their own mental filters—unless they are given enough context to understand what the actual intent of the message is.

Below are some of the dangers of employees running into frequent misunderstandings:

- **Unstable working environment.** Poor communication makes it difficult to collaborate on tasks, plan and execute goals, and resolve conflict in a positive way. Employees may feel like they are walking on eggshells when communicating with each other, which prevents them from being honest and holding each other accountable.

- **Frequent workplace conflict.** It is typical to have ongoing conflict when employees aren't able to communicate effectively with each other. The conflict is caused by wrong assumptions being made about employees' intentions and behaviors. Moreover, team members may have unspoken expectations that they hold each other accountable to. When these expectations aren't met, it could be seen as a sign of disrespect or power struggles.

- **Culture of distrust and suspicion.** Gossip and backstabbing are vicious behaviors that occur within teams whenever there are unaddressed issues caused by misunderstandings. Instead of being direct and proactive about resolving conflict, false narratives are created and spread amongst team members. This habit creates a "me vs. them" mentality where employees feel reluctant to trust coworkers.

Good communication doesn't just happen. It is a skill that must be taught and reinforced on a continuous basis within teams.

WHAT IS OPEN COMMUNICATION?

Communication is at the core of healthy relationships, but not all communication is effective. There are many times when messages are misunderstood or delivered in an inappropriate manner, leading to negative outcomes.

Open communication is a direct and transparent style of delivering messages that reduces ambiguity or passive-aggressive communication. The messages could be pleasant or unpleasant, but either way, they are conveyed clearly and assertively.

The reason open communication is effective in a team environment is that it respects the unique beliefs and perspectives of every team member and provides a platform to articulate them without feeling judged. There are no right or wrong solutions, feedback, or opinions with open communication because every individual's contribution is valid.

Open communication is not only the key to organizational success; it is the secret to happy and healthy teams. When employees can share their thoughts without hesitation, raise concerns with each other, and negotiate a way forward, they can solve problems quicker and achieve team goals. In this type of collaborative environment, employees feel safe to disagree and take ownership of their work.

Another benefit of open communication is the power to facilitate honest conversations. In diverse, multiracial, and multicultural teams, it is crucial for employees to be able to express ideas without feeling afraid to step on coworkers' toes. Honest conversations allow employees to be vulnerable with each other and share their strengths and weaknesses. The intention behind these conversations is to learn rather than impose one's own beliefs and expectations.

Of course, it takes a great deal of trust and courage to reach this level of openness. Having regular open discussions about tough topics is one way of encouraging honest conversations. Instead of avoiding certain sensitive topics that affect employees, you can create a psychologically safe environment for the topics to be discussed, and teams can collaborate on possible solutions.

If you are looking for ways to introduce honest conversations to your team, here are a few communication exercises to encourage:

Accept That You Have Needs and Preferences

Employees can often second guess what they think or feel. They may worry about being perceived negatively for sharing their ideas or concerns. This leads to passive or passive-aggressive communication, where real feelings and intentions are concealed.

It is important to remind employees through dialogue that it is okay to express needs and preferences. For instance, in a meeting, you can ask each person, "How do you feel about this?" or "What are your thoughts on this topic?"

Even though teams are trained to work toward collaborative goals, they are not required to think or feel the same way about ideas. It is okay for them to express discomfort or disapproval when they have reasons to object.

Use "I Feel... I Need" Statements

Continuing from the first point, you can encourage employees to use the simple "I feel... I need" statement to share their unique perspectives. The statement is designed to help them identify their take on a situation and proactively solve the problem.

For example, if an employee feels left out of discussions pertaining to a project, they can use the statement to raise their concerns and offer suggestions. They might say, "I feel isolated from the rest of the group. I need more information so I can contribute to discussions."

Notice how this statement bypasses adverse emotional reactions. The reason for this is because emotional outbursts distract from the core issues. By going the honest route and sharing exactly how they feel and what they need, employees can address problems before they grow and become worse.

Practice Honest Conversations Around Low-Stakes Topics

If your team is still learning to trust each other and are not yet ready to have conversations around diversity and inclusion, you can help them get comfortable sharing different perspectives by raising low-stake topics.

For example, during feedback sessions, you can ask teams to share their thoughts on the everyday office processes and how they might improve. Make sure the topics are impersonal so that employees can share their ideas and experiences without fear of judgment.

Another fun way to get employees to open up is to ask them questions about their personal lives, such as their likes, dislikes, and desires in life. These are also low-stake topics that are non-threatening and enable employees to get to know one another.

Learning to have honest conversations can strengthen open communication between employees. But what exactly does it take to engage honestly? We have already mentioned factors like trust and courage, but the core skill employees will need to learn is emotional intelligence.

HOW EMOTIONAL INTELLIGENCE CAN FACILITATE OPEN COMMUNICATION

Emotional intelligence (EQ) is the ability to recognize and understand your emotions, as well as the emotions of others. But moreover, it is the intelligence to know how to respond emotionally in different types of situations. EQ makes it possible to discern between what you are feeling and what is happening in reality. In most cases, people confuse the two and react based on their emotions instead of logically assessing the situation.

Managers and leaders at large are advised to develop EQ, but teams can benefit from learning this skill too. When employees are able to communicate with EQ, they can separate their feelings from team objectives and goals, look for win-win outcomes when resolving conflict, and focus on adjusting their behaviors to promote the interests of the whole team.

For example, EQ allows an employee to recognize how their lateness to work negatively affects coworkers. It could lead to task delays, wasted time, and miscommunication between teams. Thus, to prevent these consequences, they might work on arriving at work at the expected hour.

Someone without EQ may have felt personally attacked for being called out on their lateness. As a defense mechanism, they may have created excuses or blamed other people or things for arriving late. This type of response would make it difficult for them to see how their behaviors affect others and willingly take accountability.

EQ can be a game-changer when addressing issues of workplace inequality. Since this issue is a sensitive one and can be triggering to employees who are impacted, it is crucial to discuss cases of inequality in a calm and controlled manner. EQ can help employees control intense emotions and ensure they don't get in the way of having constructive conversations about workplace inequality. As a result, these issues can be addressed professionally without compromising work relationships.

An employee without EQ might throw a tantrum, make false allegations, or use inappropriate words and behaviors to express their anger. Even though they may be justified in feeling angry, they must maintain professionalism at work and avoid violating the rights of others. EQ makes it possible to engage with coworkers you dislike or raise sensitive issues while showing respect and self-control.

If you dream of having a team with high EQ, you can start by teaching them three key skills that can improve their ability to manage strong emotions and empathize with the emotions of others. These skills include:

Self-Awareness

Self-awareness is the ability to reflect on your inner world. This skill forms the foundation of EQ because it helps you understand the connection between thoughts, emotions, and behaviors. Essentially, your perceptions trigger specific emotions and drive you to take action. By adjusting how you perceive certain situations, you can ultimately trigger different emotions and actions.

More than recognizing what you are thinking and feeling, self-awareness causes you to see that not everybody will share the same perception of reality as you. How you view the work environment has a lot to do with prior experiences of work, and other sociocultural factors, like the challenges of finding equitable and inclusive workplaces for people of color.

Therefore, not every colleague will feel as passionate about certain issues as you or interpret certain practices as forms of discrimination. This means that you cannot expect coworkers to instinctively know when their actions have offended you. As people who think and feel differently from you, they must be educated on how to respond to your needs and respect boundaries.

In order to help employees develop self-awareness, they must be reminded to take ownership of how they think and feel. Their thoughts and emotions are unique to their work experiences and should not be seen as universal. Moreover, employees must be encouraged to weigh the strengths and limitations of their thoughts and emotions since how they perceive the work environment may not always match the reality of what is happening.

For example, a female employee working in a team of predominantly male employees may be quick to assume her colleagues are patronizing when asking questions about her work tasks. This thought may or may not be indicative of what is happening in reality and, therefore, should be scrutinized.

Before raising the concern, she must weigh the strengths and limitations of her assumption. Could it be true that her team members are patronizing? Or has she created an unconscious bias against male employees? Would the questions have a different landing if they were asked by women colleagues?

To develop self-awareness, employees should be capable of monitoring and challenging their thoughts and emotions so they can come as close to actually seeing things for how they are rather than what they perceive them to be. A few exercises that can help employees practice self-awareness are:

- Journal about work experiences.
- Learn about coworkers' cultures and unique backgrounds.
- Pay attention to situations at work that trigger strong emotions or negative thoughts.
- Regularly ask for constructive feedback.
- Focus on the positive qualities and behaviors of coworkers or the positive values and moments experienced in the team.

Self-Regulation

Self-awareness improves your ability to regulate how you react to situations. The benefit is being able to choose responses that strengthen your work relationships instead of gradually breaking them down. It is worth mentioning again that employees are allowed to feel negative emotions about people or circumstances at work, but they have full responsibility for choosing how to manage those emotions.

Disagreements are common in all types of relationships, including work relationships. Self-regulation teaches you how to express thoughts and feelings in a controlled way to avoid exacerbating conflict. Through the skillful choice of words, gestures, and behaviors, you can diffuse tension and seek to find common ground with difficult colleagues.

When teaching employees self-regulation skills, encourage them to drop the "me vs. them" mentality. The issue with seeing coworkers as enemies or competitors is that you are more likely to respond to them in defensive or aggressive ways rather than trying to understand where they are coming from. Teach employees to see differences in culture, personalities, or working styles as something to learn from and possibly adopt instead of something to reject or undermine.

Furthermore, employees can display higher self-regulation when they are taught various ways to manage stress and anxiety. Thus, part of your strategy should include teaching them how to respond in crisis situations, solve complex problems as a team, and prioritize their well-being at work through boundary-setting and time-management skills. A few exercises that can help employees improve self-regulation are:

- Practice taking time outs or rest breaks.

- Look at challenges as growth opportunities.
- Show curiosity when they don't understand the motives of colleagues.
- Ask open-ended questions to gain a better understanding of other people's perspectives.
- Pause before sharing thoughts and feelings and recognizing they have a choice of how to respond.

Empathy

Empathy is the ability to step out of your experience and seek to understand the experiences of others. The purpose of this is to see the situation from multiple perspectives and recognize how the same factors might impact people differently.

Many decades ago, empathy was seen as an inappropriate skill in the workplace due to a prevailing culture of authoritarian leadership. It didn't matter how employees felt about practices at work; they simply had to do whatever the supervisor or manager instructed. Work environments were designed to reduce the sharing of feedback that went against organizational norms or practices.

Nowadays, organizations practice egalitarian leadership where their employees are treated as equals and there are little to no barriers to communication across structures. Managers and leaders take on a mentoring role and encourage employees to share feedback on ways to improve the working environment.

Empathy thrives in this type of work environment because the needs and experiences of workers matter to those in power. In order to achieve company or team goals, every team member must feel valued and supported. Thus, teams become a safe space to disagree, debate, and negotiate outcomes in non-threatening ways.

An important piece of advice to teach employees about being empathetic toward others is to pause whenever they start to take things personally. What others think or how they feel should not be internalized and seen as an attack on them as people. Having a difference of opinion should be treated as an opportunity to expand their minds and learn how to look at problems differently. Particularly in multicultural groups, team members may have a multitude of ideas and opinions on how to approach challenges, which stem from their diverse backgrounds.

Taking things to heart is a sign that employees are identifying too much with their own perspective and not allowing enough room for team members to add to the discussion and potentially reveal hidden opportunities.

A few exercises that can help employees improve empathy are:

- Be willing to be wrong or admit that you don't have all the answers.
- Be comfortable asking for advice and incorporating other people's ideas into improving the quality of projects.
- Learn how to listen without the intention to rebut, explain, or challenge another person's opinion.
- Get into the habit of speaking to different people in the company and learning about what they do.
- Try to imagine yourself in the position of a colleague who is of a different race, ethnicity, gender, or culture than you.

Teams with strong EQ skills are not only productive, but they create a positive environment at work. Employees look forward to meetings, collaborations, or tackling problems because of the level of acceptance and openness they receive from peers. Even awkward work situations that have the potential to divide teams can be resolved collectively.

TEAM BUILDING EXERCISE

Provide sheets of paper and pens to every team member. Ask them to draw a table with two columns. The first column should be titled "I am..." and the second column, "I am not..." In the middle of the two columns, ask them to write a big "BUT." Give the team a few minutes to complete as many statements as possible using the "I am, but I am not" format. For example, "I am a woman, but I am not a pushover at work" or "I am in my 50s, but I am not afraid of technology."

This is an opportunity to open up about themselves and shutter any misconceptions or stereotypes. Allow each person to read their statements aloud and offer a brief explanation to provide context.

IN SUMMARY

Open communication is what cultivates healthy relationships among teams. It enables employees to share thoughts and feelings without feeling scared to offend others. In diverse teams, there will inevitably be a difference in personalities and perspectives; however, being able to have honest conversations and approach issues with emotional intelligence can reduce the likelihood of conflict or misunderstandings.

Share 3 crucial strategies that will transform companies from "surviving" into "thriving"!

"We are greater than, and greater for, the sum of us."

— HEATHER MCGHEE

Having a dynamic, effective DEI policy at work is no longer simply about attracting top talent or maintaining your company's reputation. Quite simply, without it, the continuity of your organization is at risk.

Just think about it—groups once deemed "minorities" may reach majority status by 2045. What's more, diverse companies increase their revenue by 19%, and three out of every four job-seekers want to work for a diverse company. That's a lot to take in!

If you are currently formulating your DEI strategy, you certainly aren't alone. Three out of every four companies believe DEI is a priority. As aware as companies are of the importance of change, many still lack the tools to effect real change.

By this stage of your reading, you know that there are three crucial pillars (the three Cs) of effective DEI policies. You are already deep into the first C—open communication—and you know the dangers that misunderstandings can wreak on your organization.

You also know how important honesty is. You can have the most sophisticated, statistically proven components of a sound DEI program in your office, but if you're not willing to listen to the people who work for you, then you cannot expect to progress.

You are aware of the importance of your ideas, behaviors, and outlook. Without self-awareness and self-regulation, it is practically impossible to connect with employees and create an atmosphere in which they are secure and confident enough to give you feedback—one of the most important pieces of the DEI puzzle.

If this book has the ideas you need to shake up your DEI policy and bring it in line with the zeitgeist, please leave a quick review on Amazon.

Let other leaders know that DEI isn't a mysterious or impenetrable wall.

By listening to their employees, working alongside them, and formulating clear, impactful, collaborative goals, companies can achieve authentic internal and external change.

Thank you so much for your support. My aim is to make a real difference, not only to managers but also to employees who have a profound need for their voices to be heard.

Scan the QR code below

COMMUNICATE (THE CRISP WAY)

In teamwork, silence isn't golden, it's deadly.

— MARK SANBORN

DO UNTO OTHERS AS YOU WOULD HAVE THEM DO UNTO YOU

Growing up, we are taught a moral principle known as the golden rule. The golden rule states: Do unto others as you would have them do unto you (Shoobridge, 2020). Each culture and religion will have its own adaptation of this rule; however, the principle is the same. Implementing this rule in the playground may be effective for preventing fights between children, but would it have the same effect in a professional environment? The answer is yes, but there would need to be exceptions to the rule.

Before we look at the exceptions, let us discuss what the instruction means. Doing unto others what you would have them do unto you simply asks you to be mindful of how you treat others. It calls upon skills like self-awareness and empathy to be able to assess the impact of your words and actions.

The assumption made is that you wouldn't tolerate being treated poorly; thus, you should be cautious not to treat your employees poorly. Even though, as a manager or leader, you may have more power and flexibility than other employees; this doesn't give you the right to disempower others.

With that being said, this rule can sometimes create a bit of confusion when managing a diverse team. How can a manager of a particular race, culture, or gender treat employees from diverse backgrounds the same way he or she wants to be treated? Wouldn't that disregard the needs and preferences of each employee?

Just imagine a sarcastic boss communicating with sarcasm whenever conveying messages. As much as they enjoy the humor and believe it makes communication entertaining, other employees may not see it that way. Or what would happen if a white manager resolved a race dispute between employees by considering what he or she would have done or said in that situation? Would that be a good display of empathy and self-awareness? Certainly not.

Therefore, there are many times when it is inappropriate to approach situations as you would ideally prefer them to be. Sometimes, you will need to approach them as others would ideally prefer them to be. In other words, instead of "doing unto others what you would have them do unto you," the better approach would be "doing unto others what they themselves would do."

The alternative statement is an exception to the rule. It is most useful when leading diverse teams and chances are high that employees will have different needs and expectations. For example, in multiracial, multicultural, and multi-gendered teams, each employee expects situations to be handled differently. They come from different backgrounds and have unique pressures that they experience at work. Thus, treating them how they themselves want to be treated promotes equity and ensures that all employees feel seen and heard.

Linking it back to communication, employees will most likely have different communication needs and preferences. Some may prefer a direct and instructional approach, while others may expect more back-and-forth and sharing of ideas. Having to adapt your communication style to each employee would be time-consuming. The best solution is to learn how to communicate assertively so that you are able to convey messages clearly while being open and accepting of different perspectives.

THE BRIDGE BETWEEN PASSIVE AND AGGRESSIVE COMMUNICATION

Assertive communication is the universal language that employees from diverse backgrounds respond positively to. What makes this form of communication so effective is the fact that it promotes openness and empathy while being very clear about expectations.

As a manager, you will need to continuously engage with employees and ensure that everyone on the team feels comfortable. But since you are the leader steering the ship, you cannot interact with employees as though they are friends. Assertive communication is a non-judgmental, straightforward style of delivering messages that considers the needs of others. It is the perfect blend between passive and aggressive communication.

Passive communication is agreeable and permissive. Managers who adopt this style of communication have a difficult time enforcing boundaries and holding teams accountable to work expectations. When there are disputes among teams, they may attempt to downplay the seriousness of the matters and avoid issuing consequences for actions. As a result, employees may lose respect for them and start to govern teams on their own, which creates smaller factions within teams and ongoing conflict.

Aggressive communication takes the complex opposite approach. Instead of being agreeable and permissive, aggressive managers are inflexible and restrictive. They tend to have certain expectations about how employees should behave at work and ignore the fact that employees have needs and preferences too. The only boundaries they recognize and respect are those they set themselves, which means they are capable of violating their employees' boundaries. Employees tend to lose respect for these types of managers as well because they come across as bullies.

Assertive communication is based on mutual respect and understanding. It takes a diplomatic approach to resolving disputes and responding to employee needs. In diverse teams, being assertive can help you build trust with employees and show confidence in yourself as a leader. Of course, there will still be times when offenses occur or teams run into misunderstandings. However, conflict can be addressed with respect, curiosity, and openness. Instead of the "me vs. them" mentality, teams can develop an "us vs. the problem" mentality.

Learning how to become an assertive leader takes time and practice. If you desire to improve your assertive communication skills or train your team to become assertive communicators, you can start practicing the CRISP communication method.

WHAT IS "THE CRISP WAY?"

Assertive communication is a tool that allows you to communicate messages with clarity and conviction. However, it doesn't take away the discomfort of having tough conversations, such as discussing issues related to DEI.

Even the most confident employee may shuffle in their seat and murmur inaudible words when the topic of DEI is raised. Unfortunately, there is no getting around the fact that this is a topic that many employees aren't willing to talk openly about.

The CRISP communication method is a technique that can help both employers and employees tackle difficult conversations without compromising the unity within their teams. The acronym stands for clear, respectful, inclusive, sincere, and prompt. Structuring communication according to the CRISP method can prevent three common problems that occur whenever the topic of DEI is brought up:

Denial

Some employees go into a state of denial when the topic of DEI is raised. They become defensive and fail to acknowledge how the impact of existing social structures like race and gender impact employees at work. Some may even go as far as denying a need for more inclusion and representation, citing that inequalities don't exist. For someone who is in denial, the lack of inclusivity or representation isn't a company issue but rather the failure of individuals to make more of an effort to assimilate into the existing culture.

Here are statements that show a denial of the issue of DEI:

- "You're making things up. There is no racism in this organization."
- "There is no such thing as marginalized employees. Everybody is treated equally."
- "Blame women for choosing to have babies and neglecting their career development."

Disengagement

There are also groups of employees who may recognize a need for DEI initiatives but excuse themselves from taking part and providing feedback. In other words, they don't necessarily disagree like those in denial, but they don't feel the urge to take action or speak up for marginalized coworkers. Their disengagement could be caused by a lack of education around DEI and how it affects teams at large, or they may fear retaliation if they openly speak against discriminatory practices at work.

Here are some statements that show disengagement about the issue of DEI:

- "I support the need for DEI initiatives, but I'm too busy to attend training."
- "Yes, I witnessed a racist remark being made but I didn't want to add fuel to the fire, so I kept quiet."
- "Sure, this is a big problem. However, it is not something I want to discuss in a professional environment."

Derailing

Derailing can be a counterproductive behavior practiced by a few employees who are part of the dominant

COMMUNICATE (THE CRISP WAY) | 93

group at work. For instance, they could be a group of male employees in a male-dominated team or company. They seek to derail focus from DEI initiatives by invalidating the experiences of marginalized groups. The purpose of this behavior is to protect the interests of the dominant group and maintain the status quo.

Here are statements that show derailing from the issue of DEI:

- "Employees who claim to be marginalized want special treatment."
- "The gender-based income gap is a conspiracy created by greedy female workers."
- "Nobody considers how many challenges the dominant group faces. This is starting to feel like reverse discrimination."

When employees are in a state of denial, disengagement, or derailment, they are not able to actively participate in DEI initiatives and be part of the change. But even more, they are unable to show emotional intelligence around matters that affect their peers.

Assertive communication, by way of practicing the CRISP method, can help those who are for or against DEI voice their thoughts and feelings in a constructive manner that encourages dialogue. Remember, assertive communication is based on mutual respect, not agree-ableness. Thus, even team members who are on different sides of the debate can engage with each other on this topic while maintaining civility.

The following sections will outline the five components of CRISP. If you intend on teaching this method to your team, introduce one component at a time, and spend several months practicing it. When you believe they have a good command of the component, intro-duce the next one, and so on.

Clear

The first component of CRISP communication is being clear about your intended message. Your ideas should be carefully packaged so that the listener doesn't need to think deeply about what you mean. In other words, the words and phrases you use must make sense.

Vague messages leave room for misunderstandings. It is always better for coworkers to know where you stand on a matter than to assume the worst. Bear in mind that clear communication isn't rude or negative. It is simple and easy to understand. Note that you can disagree without being offensive, but more on respect and sincerity later!

For now, you will need to remember the following points:

Seek to Be Understood, Not Approved

Whenever you are sharing messages with employees or they are sharing messages with each other, the aim should be to leave the conversation feeling understood. There may not always be a unanimous agreement on an idea or suggestion, but that shouldn't be the goal.

In order for employees to weigh in on what you are communicating, they must first understand what you mean. Focus on helping them understand the context and intentions behind your messages so that they don't fill the gaps of knowledge with their own assumptions. It is okay if they disagree once they have understood your message. After all, disagreements are opportunities for problem-solving and coming up with better ideas.

Consider the Environment

Sometimes the number one cause of confusion isn't the actual message itself but where, when, and to whom the message is spoken to. Imagine an employee raising a concern about the loose bathroom faucets in the middle of a strategy meeting. Even though the concern is valid, the timing and setting for the message are inappropriate.

Every form of feedback is valuable to the organization, but there is a time and place to have these conversations. Some of the questions to ask yourself before bringing up an issue include:

- Have I chosen the right words?
- Have I chosen the right time?
- Am I initiating the conversation at the right place?
- Am I sharing the message with the right person?
- Am I delivering the message in the best way?

By screening your message against these questions, you will reduce the likelihood of confusion and ensure that what you have to say is received in the best possible way.

Anticipate Objections and Questions

Before sharing your message, consider possible objections and questions. This will help you refine the message and make it as simple as possible. It also allows you to imagine the various ways others might interpret what you have to say and if there could be groups of employees who feel offended.

Remember the exception to the golden rule? Treat others as they themselves would want to be treated.

When creating messages, picture how the listener reacts after hearing what you have to say. Without changing your main idea or intention, go back and rephrase the message to avoid any negative comments and reactions.

If you like, you can go the extra mile and create a sheet of possible questions the listener or audience may ask and see whether your message provides answers to those questions. If not, rephrase the message to provide as much context as possible so that there are few clarifying questions posed.

Please note that you don't need to be an expert on the topic you are sharing to express clear messages. You only need to be certain about what you want to say and find the simplest way to say it. For example, you may not know a lot about African American history but wish to convey your support for African American employees and the challenges they may be facing. Here is how you might structure your message:

"I am not African American and do not know enough about your culture to comment on matters affecting you at work. However, I would like to show solidarity by openly expressing my support for you."

This type of message starts out with a disclaimer to show respect and sensitivity toward the struggles of other employees. It also clarifies any questions about the speaker's position on the matter. While they may not be a decision-maker, they are in support of initiatives that might help affected employees.

Respectful

The second component of CRISP communication is being respectful. Since respect means something different for each employee, it can be difficult to enforce a standard at work. However, a great theme to focus on is celebrating the differences of others.

When teams have a positive attitude toward coworkers' differences, they can be more open and respectful of who they are and their needs and desires in a work environment. For example, when white managers commit to understanding how being systematically disadvantaged in the workplace affects the attitudes and sense of belonging for people of color, they can show greater willingness to listen to their concerns and treat feedback as opportunities for learning.

Celebrating the differences of others may even extend to encouraging inclusive language in conversation. For example, to make members of the LGBTQIA+ community feel represented at work, you can encourage the team to add pronouns to their email signatures or Slack profiles so others are aware of how to refer to them. Another example is addressing coworkers by their full names and seeking clarity on pronunciation when the names are not common. This kind of inclusive language demonstrates respect and shows a willingness to make space for different types of people at work.

There are three points to remember when seeking to show respect during conversations, especially to coworkers who may come from different racial, class, or cultural backgrounds. These include:

Use "I" Messages

One way to show respect is by distinctively separating your ideas from another person's through taking ownership. Using "I" statements, such as "I think" and "I feel," show a separation between the opinions presented by others and your own. Doing this allows you to disagree or add to the discussion without invalidating what the other person has already contributed.

It also allows you to reflect on your own thoughts and feelings without feeling compelled to take on someone else's perspective. Remember, disagreements are unavoidable when employees from diverse backgrounds are brought together. It's not whether you disagree or not that matters, but how you navigate these disagreements.

Spend More Time Listening Than Speaking

There is power in listening more than speaking. When you stop what you are doing and actively listen to what someone else is communicating, you are able to listen for meaning and understanding instead of listening to respond. This means less time going back and forth to clarify intentions and more time spent exchanging and building upon ideas.

In today's world, we are often pressured to do everything quickly, including rushing crucial conversations. However, when we are focused on having quick conversations, we are unable to fully grasp the message being conveyed, thereby wasting valuable time.

In many cultures, active listening is a sign of respect. You don't necessarily have to agree with what is being said for the other person to feel respected. By making eye contact, showing interest, and engaging with their message, they feel acknowledged.

There are three types of questions you can ask to show that you are listening to the speaker and value their message:

- **Clarifying questions:** These questions seek to gain a better understanding of the intention behind the words and phrases and the message as a whole. They may start with "Do you mean...?" or "Are you saying that...?"

- **Probing questions:** Once you understand the gist of what is being said, you can ask probing questions to request more information. You might say, "When you say... what do you mean?" or "Why is this topic important to you?"

- **Confirming questions:** To ensure that you have understood the full message, you can confirm what you heard being shared. For instance, you might say, "If I am understanding you correctly, you are saying..." or "Am I correct to say that you feel...?"

- **Watch your nonverbal cues:** Another point to remember when communicating respectfully is to monitor your nonverbal cues. These are the messages you convey through specific gestures, facial expressions, or body language. It is estimated that over 70% of your communication is nonverbal. As such, your words either confirm or contradict what your body displays. For example, sitting with your arms and legs crossed at a DEI meeting shows disengagement. You might express support with your words but these are contradicted by your actions. The same applies to making certain gestures like pointing at the speaker or rolling your eyes. These cues convey a negative message about how you feel toward the speaker or about the topic being discussed.

Therefore, during team discussions, specifically when sensitive topics are brought up, check in with yourself. Take a moment to observe your body language and whether it is communicating a positive attitude. It may also help to practice speaking about sensitive topics while looking at yourself in the mirror. Notice cues like your tone of voice, use of hands, or facial expressions. Assess whether your delivery of the message conveys acceptance.

Inclusive

The third component of CRISP communication is being inclusive. While using inclusive language is one way of encouraging inclusive communication, the focus should be on making sure that employees feel a sense of belonging in the workplace.

For example, you can emphasize the importance of feedback and, through action, show employees that their voices matter. Having different communication channels available for employees to share different ideas and thoughts can also enhance a sense of belonging.

For example, there could be a channel for sharing praise and good news and another to raise workplace issues and improvements. You could also create an anonymous channel where employees can submit feedback without revealing identifying information. This offers protection to marginalized employees who may be afraid of being victimized for sharing their truth.

Inclusive communication also places importance on engaging everyone at all levels of the company. Some companies go as far as incentivizing employee participation. For example, employees could earn points or rewards for completing questionnaires, joining DEI training or initiatives, and bringing innovative ideas forward. The purpose of putting so much emphasis on participation is to help employees understand the door is always open. They are always welcome to be a part of the ongoing conversation or change processes taking place at work.

As much as teams attempt to be inclusive in everything they do, many still get it wrong. The reason for that is employees practice inclusive communication without self-awareness. Before using inclusive language or creating another promoting participation, encourage employees to reflect on their power and privilege. This simple exercise provides an opportunity to check their own thought processes and emotions and imagine how their message would be received.

Every employee has power and rank—even entry-level employees have some measure of power and rank in comparison to others. We can define power as the amount of authority an employee holds in a company and rank as the level of superiority or inferiority they feel compared to coworkers. The higher the rank employees have, the more power they enjoy, either among teams or across the organization. Some of the factors that influence ranking include race, gender, culture, education, professional network, job position, associations, and so on.

The people who are more acutely aware and sensitive to rank issues are employees who don't have much of it. This explains why they are more likely to have conflict with employees who have a high rank. Nobody wants to feel inferior to another human being, especially when the rank has not been earned. For instance, a highly educated woman who has more work experience than a man working in a lower position may feel frustrated at the fact that the man is able to advance quicker in their career and land more work opportunities simply because they were born male.

Bringing it back to inclusive communication, it is important to teach employees to be mindful of their power and rank when conveying messages because sometimes what they say can be interpreted negatively, despite them having good intentions. For the mere fact that they have more power and rank than the individual they are communicating with, the message won't be received as intended.

Thus, if possible, it is good for employees to adjust communication depending on who they are speaking to. This level of sensitivity makes a significant difference in how messages are exchanged and received among employees.

Please note that since everybody has a measure of power and rank, it shouldn't be something you feel guilty about. Nevertheless, it is a sign of emotional intelligence to be conscious of the privilege you hold at work and to use that privilege consciously.

Sincere

So far, we have discussed the need for employees to be clear, respectful, and inclusive in the way they communicate with one another. However, without sincerity, the message can be lost in translation. What makes a message impactful isn't so much what is said but how it is communicated.

In a quote, author George Orwell describes the importance of sincere communication. He says, "The great enemy of clear language is insincerity. When there is a gap between one's real and one's declared aims, one turns as it were instinctively to long words and exhausted idioms, like a cuttlefish spurting out ink" (Bilanich, 2009, para. 4).

What we can take from the quote is that the lack of sincerity causes unclear communication. Since you are not connected to what you are saying, you are unable to express genuine thoughts and feelings. In other words, you might say what you think employees want to hear, not what you believe strongly.

Insincerity is the enemy of open communication. It prevents honest conversations from taking place and conflict from being addressed and resolved. For example, during a feedback session, a team member makes a sarcastic comment about an issue another colleague is going through.

The comment creates tension between the two members and distracts from the agenda of the session, which is to seek honest feedback. When those insincere comments aren't stopped, it could cause employees to shut down and not take the process of giving feedback seriously.

Being sincere is about being genuine about how you feel, even if your emotions aren't pleasant. It is about believing your words and not just saying them for the sake of it. Employees can intuitively sense when their coworkers or leaders are being insincere. There is a strange coldness or dullness in their words or body language, which makes their "positive" message ineffective.

Since sincerity requires authenticity, you cannot teach employees to be sincere. For example, if members of the dominant group at work are convinced that there is no such thing as marginalization or unequal practices, they cannot fake being in support of DEI initiatives. Instead, what you can do as a manager is encourage employees to share their thoughts and feelings honestly, even if they are controversial. Being honest is a display of sincerity because your messages reflect where you stand on a matter.

You can also introduce employees to a concept known as common humanity. Common humanity recognizes that although we may have many differences, there are undeniable qualities and experiences that unite us, one of them being the desire to belong. Regardless of the skin color, gender, or ranking of employees, they all desire to find a workplace where they belong.

Focusing on qualities and experiences that cause employees to relate with one another can inspire cooperation and sincere conversations. They may even be motivated to work toward a culture that incorporates shared values and interests, one that is both equal and equitable.

Prompt

The fifth component of CRISP communication is being prompt, which means getting to the point quickly rather than beating around the bush. Promptness is closely tied to clarity because when your message is straightforward, you are able to deliver it quickly.

Nonetheless, the word "prompt" can also be used as a verb to mean provoking a certain response from someone. When you share a message with a team, you prompt them to reflect on what was said and respond with the appropriate actions. Depending on how you deliver the message, the prompt could evoke a positive or negative response.

For example, if you fail to choose your words wisely when addressing angry employees about a recent conflict that occurred in the team, your message may add fuel to the fire and widen the rift between team members. It is important to be mindful that what you say and how you convey the message can either serve to bring your team together or exacerbate ongoing challenges.

To ensure that you are prompting positive behaviors, always consider the final outcome. Think about how you would like employees to walk away feeling after the meeting or feedback session. You can teach the same advice to your team. Before they engage with one another about a sensitive topic or conflictual situation, ask them to take a moment and consider the final outcome. What do they want to achieve by having the discussion? How do they envision their relationship becoming better because of it?

Thinking about that final outcome allows you to carefully choose your words and behaviors, so you can avoid sending the wrong message. If you desire to prompt a positive reaction, you will need to consciously start the discussion with a positive mindset. It may even help to visualize the conversation before it happens. Envision it going in a positive direction and all parties walking away feeling seen and heard.

Before sitting down for a tough conversation like addressing DEI issues, take 10 minutes to write down your intentions for the meeting. Mention what would need to happen for the meeting to go well; what topics would need to be addressed? What resolutions would need to take place? And how would all parties need to walk away feeling?

At the meeting, right after exchanging pleasantries, ask the parties what their intentions are for the discussion too. Go through the same questions and note their responses on a piece of paper. Place all of your intentions at the center of the table and ask each person to be mindful of their own intentions, as well as to hold other people in the room accountable. This short exercise will ensure that everyone is cautious of their attitudes and behaviors in order to make the appropriate prompts.

TEAM BUILDING EXERCISE

Host a "Speak your truth" session where the team comes together and speaks about issues that have been swept under the rug. Before the session starts, lay down some ground rules, such as whatever is shared must be kept among the team, no interrupting while someone is speaking, and validate what the speaker said before responding, and so on.

Assign one person on the team to be the scribe, taking down minutes of the topics discussed and resolutions that were suggested. Before ending the session, agree on the next date when you will come together and evaluate if any improvements have been made. Make these sessions voluntary and include a trigger warning on the invite in case there are sensitive topics brought up that make employees feel uncomfortable.

IN SUMMARY

Conversations around DEI require assertive communication that is both clear and considerate of other people's feelings. One of the ways to improve your assertive communication skills is by practicing the CRISP method. CRISP is an acronym that stands for clear, respectful, inclusive, sincere, and prompt. Each component of the acronym offers an effective way of packaging and delivering messages across teams. While the CRISP method won't make DEI conversation less difficult to have, it will ensure that employees are able to exchange ideas and respect each other's viewpoints, even when they don't share the same perspectives.

THE SECRET SAUCE TO INCLUSIVITY

Find a group of people who challenge and inspire you, spend a lot of time with them, and it will change your life.

— AMY POEHLER

WHY SOME EMPLOYEES DISLIKE COLLABORATION

If you ask any leader to describe their ideal work environment, they will mention the word collaboration at some point. The reason leaders seem to be so passionate about collaboration is due to the level of engagement and performance employees are capable of displaying when working together on tasks or shared goals.

However, the mention of collaboration doesn't excite many employees. When they think of teamwork, they are transported back to school days when there was an unequal distribution of tasks, and they had to chase peers down just to complete projects on time. Those memories still haunt employees, making them less enthusiastic about collaboration.

A study completed at the University of Phoenix found that 75% of people would prefer not to work in teams, and 70% of people specifically did not want to work in dysfunctional teams (Jackson, 2017). Unfortunately, with the way the global workforce is heading, teamwork is fast becoming the preferred method of carrying out company goals. This means that managers must be open to understanding what might cause resistance to collaboration and how to make employees feel more positive about working together.

First, let us look at some of the common reasons employees are against or hesitant about teamwork:

- Employees fear not being able to keep up with the pace of team members and therefore being blamed or looked at unfavorably for slowing them down.

- Employees don't like the idea of working closely with people they dislike or who display very different work and communication styles.
- Employees fear working in teams when there aren't clear goals and objectives outlined. In such cases, team members may create their own goals, which becomes frustrating for others.
- Employees fear working on a team without clear roles and designations. For instance, when there is poor leadership and team members don't know who to report to, usually the people with the loudest voices or opinions (who may not have the skills to lead) seek to dominate.
- Employees don't like the idea of uneven work distribution. They fear working alongside team members who need to be pushed or guided constantly in order to perform.

There are, of course, many other reasons, some of which are specific to the organization or department. If possible, sit down with employees and ask open questions about their experience working in teams. Ask them to share both positive and negative thoughts or feelings they may have about teamwork and what they believe can be done to improve collaboration.

THE IMPORTANCE OF COLLABORATION

Your task as a leader is to get employees to buy into the idea of working collectively on goals. This will ensure that everyone makes the most out of time spent solving problems, implementing strategies, and striving for company success.

When employees genuinely enjoy working together, they can transfer ideas and skills, improve communication and conflict resolution, and strengthen connections. The truth is there are a multitude of benefits to teamwork, and many of them promote diversity and representation.

Below are a few ways collaboration positively impacts DEI goals:

Employees Can Combat Loneliness

Many companies now offer work-from-home, or a hybrid work schedule, so to keep employees engaged and performing at their peak, they must promote collaboration on goals. Some companies combat employee loneliness by making collaboration an option, like providing an unstructured virtual room where employees can enter and work quietly in the presence of coworkers. Other virtual rooms can be created to have one-on-one meetings and feedback sessions with team leaders.

Employees Can Learn How to Communicate With Each Other

Oftentimes, teamwork is the only opportunity employees get to engage with each other. Therefore, when working together, they can get to know team members on a professional and personal level. In diverse companies, teamwork is a good way to promote inclusion because employees are encouraged to engage with different types of people, some of whom they have never spoken to outside of work.

Of course, when bringing different types of people together, there is the possibility of resistance to collaboration. For the most part, this is caused by unconscious biases carried by members of the team. However, the door to communicating about present challenges is open —even more than if independent employees were encouraged to speak to each other about their differences.

Solving Problems Becomes a Quick and Creative Exercise

Besides physical distance, another isolating experience is attempting to solve complex problems on your own. Although employees are competent enough to tackle challenges faced on the job, they can perform better under pressure when given support.

Collaborating on tasks allows teams to pull together their collective skills, knowledge, and experience to address work challenges. Instead of making problems the sole responsibility of one person to address, they become the team's responsibility. This alleviates stress from individuals and makes the process of problem-solving quick and interactive.

Employees Can Live Out the Company Culture

The purpose of company culture is to provide a framework for a healthy and productive work environment. What better way to enforce culture than to assign employees to teams and mentor them as they learn how to meet work expectations and interact with each other?

If there were no opportunities to meet and work collectively, employees could not live out the values of your organization. Instead, they would focus on individual goals and develop a competitive spirit with one another. Collaboration positively transforms an organization by ensuring that employees are held accountable to its mission and values.

WHAT DOES EFFECTIVE COLLABORATION LOOK LIKE?

To create a win-win situation, where both employer and employee are satisfied with the amount of collaboration taking place in the organization, teamwork needs to become something that is inclusive, provides ample support to achieve work goals, and has a positive impact on all team members.

You may be wondering what that might look like in practice. According to Asana, the workflow management app, there are a number of factors that must be present for a team to be productive, innovative, and maintain positive relationships (Asana, 2022). These include:

- **Celebrate diversity.** Nowadays, it is common to work with people from diverse backgrounds. Strong teams are able to look at the present differences as opportunities for learning new skills and perspectives. Team members are assigned tasks based on their strengths instead of their power or rank, which allows for innovative and impactful outcomes.
- **Encourage open communication.** Teams with effective collaboration value open communication. Not only does it save them a

lot of time, but it is also a way to make sure there is no gatekeeping of information or issues swept under the rug. Team members feel comfortable asking questions, debating ideas, and even expressing their concerns. A non-judgmental environment is created to give team members the platform to speak and be heard.

- **Solve problems and develop solutions together.** The best way to assess whether teams are collaborating effectively is to determine how they address challenges. Do they run to their own corners and blame colleagues for the crises? Or do they stop whatever they are working on and prioritize fixing the problems? Healthy and productive teams will often schedule regular group brainstorming sessions. While these sessions are created to solve problems and develop solutions, teams may also use them to resolve team conflict or plan and coordinate cross-functional projects. These sessions are something the entire team looks forward to because of the synergy they have created with each other.

- **Trust each other.** Another positive sign of effective collaboration is the degree of trust built by the team. Great teamwork requires each team member to manage parts of a task or project. This is different from working alone, where employees are in charge of whole tasks or projects. Trust enables team members to give up the reins and focus solely on the duties they are responsible for, having faith in their colleagues to also complete their assigned duties.

- **Hold each other accountable.** When team members trust each other, they are able to hold each other accountable to work expectations without entering conflict. They frequently check in with each other to see how everybody is holding up and whether targets or deadlines need to be adjusted. With accountability comes a measure of support. Team members are not afraid to ask for help or seek clarity on tasks. They are confident that their colleagues will help them locate and resolve issues that might affect achieving mutual goals.

Take a few moments to think about your team. How many of these factors do they display on a daily basis? And which ones do they need to work on? Your aim is to continue holding discussions and feedback sessions with your team to identify the challenges that hold them back from effectively collaborating with one another and find ways to overcome them as a unit.

TEAM BUILDING EXERCISE

Play an improvisation game to encourage team bonding. Start by writing a list of company values and desirable work practices on separate Post-it notes. Fold each note and place it inside a jar. Ask a member of the team to volunteer to start the game. They will need to pick a note from the jar and mime whatever action is written on it. Other employees should guess what is being acted out. The first person to guess correctly stands in front and starts the game all over again.

IN SUMMARY

Not every employee is excited about the idea of working closely with their colleagues. However, this unfavorable attitude toward teamwork may be caused by past experiences working in dysfunctional teams. Since collaboration offers so many benefits to an organization, it is vital to change employees' perceptions about teamwork and make it something they look forward to.

HOW TO COLLABORATE

A group becomes a team when each member is sure
enough of himself and his contribution to praise the
skills of others.

— NORMAN SHIDLE

11 WAYS TO BOOST COLLABORATIVE EFFORTS

When you don't already have a culture of collaboration, it can be difficult to get employees to buy into this concept. However, with the correct approach, you can convince employees that working together is better than working alone.

One of the key areas you will need to work on when boosting collaborative efforts is team alignment. This refers to how well the team synergizes with one another. Research from McKinsey and Company shows that 97% of employees cite a lack of team alignment as one of the factors that impact the outcome of tasks and projects (Bit.AI, 2018).

Getting a team to align on values and goals isn't an overnight process, but you can assist them by reinforcing the 11 components of the acronym COLLABORATE. Some of these components have already been discussed at length in previous chapters, so you may already be familiar with them. Others may require an open mind and willingness to step outside of your comfort zone as a leader.

Here are 11 ways to foster collaboration within your team:

C: Communicate

We have discussed the importance of open, clear, and honest communication earlier in the book. Being good communicators allows employees to improve their social skills and have more awareness of how their messages impact others.

Something worth reinforcing during team discussions is the use of inclusive language. As you know, inclusive language breaks down race, culture, gender, and sexuality barriers, making everyone feel accepted for who they are. Employees start to believe that:

1. Their beliefs and opinions matter to colleagues.
2. It is safe to discuss personal concerns and express needs.
3. Having a difference of opinion doesn't make them any less valuable on the team.

When we make examples of inclusive language, we often bring up the subject of pronouns. The truth, however, is that there are many ways to make employees feel accepted with the right choice of words. Some of them include:

- Refer to the team as "Us" and "We" instead of "You" or "Them." This simple change of possessive words can create a sense of belonging and strengthen bonds between members of a team.
- Include various options for giving and receiving feedback. If possible, try to offer online and offline methods to accommodate

employees who are tech-savvy and those who prefer traditional methods of reporting back.

- Encourage making positive assumptions about team members. For example, if an employee is late in submitting work, the rest of the team can assume they are facing a crisis and need support.
- Create an environment where employees feel safe disagreeing or drawing boundaries. This helps to strengthen trust within the team and ensure that a conflict of opinion doesn't stop them from diligently striving toward goals.

Note that a safe environment begins with words and language. Encourage employees to pause and take a few deep breaths before they speak. Unfortunately, whatever is said in anger cannot be taken back. To promote mindful communication, sit down with your team and create a list of communication rules to observe at work. Ensure that each employee has an opportunity to offer suggestions.

O: Openness

Openness can be defined as the willingness to understand others and to be understood in return. In order for this to happen, employees must put their egos to the side and seek to find commonalities among each other.

In other words, they must find what makes them similar and safe to be around.

Finding commonalities leads to openness because it removes the "Me vs. Them" narrative and replaces it with an "Us vs. Shared Goals" narrative. Plus, employees who come from diverse backgrounds are able to identify qualities about each other that transcend differences. It's not that they become color-blind or can't tell the difference between genders, but those attributes don't carry as much weight anymore.

One of the ways to practice openness is by being present in the moment. You aren't always aware when you are overly invested in your internal dialogue and how this might cause you to become rigid in your thinking. Employees may approach teamwork with the same type of absent-mindedness, which blocks them from taking part in conversations and interpreting messages without biases.

Being present is about taking regular breaks from thinking and focusing on observing what is happening in the moment. It is about cherishing each interaction with employees rather than playing back past interactions or anticipating future interactions in your mind. You don't need to think hard to embrace the moment. All that is required is to tap into your sense of sight, hearing, and touch:

- **Sight:** Look at people in their eyes when they are speaking. This is a sign of respect and indicates that you value the message being shared.
- **Hearing:** Listen attentively to the tone of voice, language, pauses, and other sounds that might help you dissect and understand the meaning of what is being communicated by others.
- **Touch:** Eliminate any physical items that might distract you from engaging with your team. For example, if you have a tendency to check your phone every five minutes for notifications, find a safe place to store your phone while participating in group discussions.

Being present in the moment can also be an opportunity to notice what is going well for the team. Take five minutes to reflect on what you are grateful for right now at work or within your team. What is currently happening that is making you satisfied with your job? For instance, do you work with patient team members? Or are you given enough support to complete tasks?

In the hustle and bustle of work life, it is easy to get into the habit of complaining about what isn't working and overlook what makes your job enjoyable. Being present can help you slow down and reflect on everyday moments that enhance your work experience.

L: Listening

We have already spoken about how active listening can be a sign of openness. But did you know that it can also be a demonstration of inclusivity?

When you show others that they have your undivided attention, it makes them feel valued. Without even verbalizing it, you convey the message: "You matter to me." It isn't necessary to agree with everything they are saying; you can maintain your own beliefs while holding space for others to share their own.

Here are some of the ways to show employees that you are listening to them:

Check Your Body Language

The first and often misunderstood sign of listening is making eye contact. Connecting to someone's eyes helps you stay focused on their message. Your mind is concentrating on a single task, which is to listen for meaning and understanding.

Besides eye contact, there are other types of positive body language that show you are listening. These include shifting your body to face the speaker, nodding to show you are following, smiling as a sign of reassurance, and mirroring their emotions (i.e., If they frown when speaking about something upsetting, you can naturally frown too, then go back to your normal expression).

Focus On Understanding the Message

When you are listening to employees, the last thing you should be thinking about is your response. This is advice you can teach employees when resolving conflict or finding ways to tackle problems as a group: Whenever a team member presents an idea or expresses their viewpoint, the focus should not be on formulating a response but rather on seeking understanding.

Listening is an opportunity to step out of your role and immerse yourself in another person's reality. Take the time to hear what they are saying and the significance of their message. Note that you won't always find yourself listening to people who validate your ideas and suggestions. Some employees may have opposing views and challenge what you have to say. However, even though their message goes against what you had intended, it is still worth listening to.

Employees may run into the same problem with their colleagues. They may assume that just because a team member presents different ideas, they are not worth paying attention to. But this isn't right. It is important to seek meaning and understanding, even in cases where ideas challenge your own; this is the best way to grow as a professional and expand your knowledge.

Summarize and Follow Up

Eventually, the speaker will conclude their thoughts and give you an opportunity to respond. Instead of jumping straight into sharing your thoughts, take a minute to summarize what you heard, and if necessary, ask follow-up questions. Not only does this indicate that you have been listening attentively, but it also shows that you care about interpreting the message correctly.

As we have already discussed in an earlier chapter, misunderstandings are caused by a lack of clarity. For instance, you may hear 60% of a message and assume you know what the 40% was alluding to. It isn't enough to understand employees partially; neither is it okay for them to partially listen to each other. Thus, summarizing what you heard and asking questions gives you a chance to confirm that you were indeed listening and understand the intention and context of the message.

Here are a few ways to summarize and follow up with questions:

- It sounds like you are unhappy with the current work schedule. Can you explain the challenges you are facing?
- What I am hearing is that you would like more support with carrying out work tasks. Did I get that right?
- From my understanding, you are having a hard time settling into the office. In what ways can I help you feel comfortable?

When you are actively listening, there will be a lot of silences. For example, you will remain silent while someone is speaking and briefly pause before responding to their message. During the silence, you should be gathering information (both verbal and nonverbal) about what is being communicated. Remind yourself that you are taking mental notes, not formulating a rebuttal.

If you are not in the physical or emotional space to give your full attention to someone, schedule another time to have the discussion. When you feel focused and attentive, you will be able to provide a more thoughtful response.

L: Learning

If you desire to boost collaboration within your team, create an incentive for learning. Propose the idea of collaboration to employees as an opportunity to stretch their thinking capacity and learn new ways to manage work or solve problems.

Every employee wants to advance in their career, but not many of them know where to start. Teamwork can be a good way to expose employees to new types of work tasks, which could inspire them to gain new skills and knowledge. The best part is that they don't need to pay for this exposure; it comes packaged in the work experiences of their team members. All they need is the willingness to step outside of their comfort zones and learn something new from others.

As a leader, you can encourage your team to have a positive attitude about learning by providing regular, constructive feedback. If possible, you can even offer instant feedback immediately after they have taken certain actions.

Instant feedback is useful because the memory of their action is still fresh in the brain, and they can easily connect how they reacted with a desirable or undesirable outcome. It also allows them to correct their mistakes on the spot, which ultimately helps them practice and reinforce their knowledge of the desired outcome.

It is also important to remember that since you are managing a diverse team, there could be employees who don't want to receive feedback regularly; they may prefer getting feedback once a month. Make a note of their preferences and treat them how they desire to be treated.

The frequency of feedback may look different for each employee, but the consistency should be the same. Commit to giving your team ongoing feedback, based on various aspects of their work life, to motivate them to keep learning and improving their performance.

Here are some tips on giving effective feedback:

Keep the Feedback Relevant

The benefit of providing ongoing feedback is that you can make each occasion specific to one aspect of the employee's work, typically the most recent action or decision they have made.

Relevant feedback supports learning because it pinpoints one task or behavior to work on. You can also provide a lot of context and examples to make it easier for the employee to correct their mistakes.

Start and End With Positive Reinforcement

Positive reinforcement is words or behaviors that feel rewarding. When parents are training children to remember desirable behaviors, they will often praise their children to reinforce the good behavior.

The same principle works in the office. Whenever you are providing feedback, start and end with positive reinforcement. Tell the employee what you are proud of and would like to see more. Hearing criticism feels less disappointing because they have been reminded of the incredible work they are doing. It is, therefore, a lot easier to correct their mistakes and look forward to receiving more compliments.

Facilitate Two-Way Feedback

If it matters to you that employees develop a love for learning, then you should be modeling the same behavior. Find ways to incorporate learning into your leadership style, such as facilitating two-way feedback. Create just as many opportunities for your team to provide feedback on your leadership. Ask them to provide suggestions on how you can improve and hold yourself accountable for taking action on their suggestions.

Knowledge is power because it empowers teams to excel at what they do. But to gain knowledge, gaps in skills and performance need to be identified and addressed. It is, therefore, beneficial to cultivate a feedback culture where your team is constantly being reviewed and encouraged to do better.

A: Accountability

Accountability in the workplace refers to the ability to take responsibility for your work and impact within the team. At any given time, employees will have a number of tasks assigned to them. They are responsible for completing those tasks at the standard set by the team and within the set deadline. They are also responsible for evaluating the quality of their work and taking the necessary action to improve their skills and knowledge.

When advertising job openings, many recruiters don't mention accountability as a required skill. This is because being accountable is perceived to be a soft skill, a professional trait that employees develop from their experience working with other people. They are either accountable for their actions or they aren't, and the difference is seen in how they approach conflict, failure, or communication issues.

There are two areas of work where accountability is crucial. The first is the day-to-day management of workflow. Managers don't have the luxury of time to chase after employees for updates and completed work. Every employee must learn how to structure their day according to work demands and ensure they are on track to meeting goals and deadlines. To demonstrate accountability, they should take ownership of their work and develop good time management skills.

Another area of work where accountability is crucial is managing conflict and communication problems. It is inevitable that employees will disagree every once in a while. The focus should not be on the fact that employees have different views but rather on how they choose to address their differences and find common ground. It takes accountability for employees to admit when they have made mistakes, jumped to conclusions, or said something that may have offended their colleagues.

Even though accountability is a skill expected from every employee, there will be some who won't take ownership of their work unless they are encouraged to by their manager. It is, therefore, necessary to practice holding your team accountable for their work tasks and everyday interactions with others. Show them through your behavior and boundaries how serious you are about meeting deadlines, producing high-quality work, treating customers well, and any other standard you hold them accountable to.

There are also a few practices you can introduce to your team that can help them become accountable. These include:

Establish Goals and Metrics Before Approaching Tasks

It can be difficult for employees to hold themselves accountable to certain work standards when they aren't sure about what they are aiming for. Encourage your team to sit down and set goals and specific objectives to measure their progress (key performance indicators).

Big goals that are expected to be reached over 6–12 months need to be broken down into smaller weekly and monthly objectives. Breaking down goals allows for more precision in the process of execution and enables the team to identify mistakes or growing issues before they become too large. Employees are also less likely to feel overworked when they can pace themselves in achieving goals.

Schedule Regular Check-Ins

You won't know how everybody is coping with work demands without regularly checking in with them. These meetings don't need to take more than 10 minutes a session. You will simply ask each employee what task they are working on, how much progress they have made, and whether they need support from you or the rest of the team. Ideally, it would be recommended to have these meetings once a week, virtually or in person.

Take Ownership of Results

When mistakes occur in a team, the common reaction is for everybody to point fingers. "If it wasn't for Mark's absenteeism," they might say, "we could have delivered the project sooner." This type of attitude causes delays, low morale, and division within the team. The better approach is for everybody to take ownership of the outcome since their actions or inactions contributed to the results.

Teach your team to see moments of failure as opportunities to reflect on their performance and ways in which they might improve in the future. Ask them to think about gaps in their own skills or knowledge that could have contributed to the failure of the team. This level of introspection promotes collaboration and taking responsibility for group outcomes rather than individual outcomes.

Building accountable teams takes a lot of patience and ongoing feedback. Your role as a leader in helping employees take initiative and strive toward shared goals is incredibly important. Model the kind of behaviors you would like employees to adopt when approaching work.

B: Building Trust

We have mentioned the importance of trust in building productive and inclusive teams. However, a question we still need to explore in detail is what trust looks like in the workplace and what it would take for employees to trust each other and the leadership.

Trust is the ability to rely on others and feel confident that they have your best interests at heart. It enables you to let down your guard and reveal your character flaws without feeling exposed. When there is a high level of trust within a team, interactions between employees feel safe and accepting. They may come from different backgrounds and hold opposite views about many work matters, but there is no sense of judgment among them.

Cultivating trust in teams doesn't start with employees —it begins with the manager or leadership team. They are in charge of creating a work atmosphere and drafting policies that make employees feel included and accepted for who they are. This type of atmosphere encourages employees to express their needs and feel confident approaching management with their concerns.

You may be wondering what a trustworthy manager looks like to an employee. Here are some common characteristics:

- **Honor their word.** A trustworthy manager never goes back on what they have said they will do. If they can't fulfill a promise, they will take accountability.
- **Friendly disposition.** A trustworthy manager is an approachable person who makes everyone feel relaxed and comfortable. They work within close proximity to their team and are available for informal and one-on-one meetings.
- **Encourages empathy.** A trustworthy manager sees employees as human beings first. They understand that outside of the work environment, their employees have lives that sometimes affect attitudes and productivity at work. They encourage team members to be kind and mindful of how they treat one another.
- **Champion progress, not perfection.** A trustworthy manager knows that employees have different working styles and performance levels. Not everybody on the team can be a high performer, and that is okay. They would rather motivate employees to continue making

progress and work on reaching achievable milestones.

- **Show respect to all employees.** A trustworthy manager understands that respect is earned, not given. They invest a lot of time in building personal relationships with each employee so that they can learn more about each other's personalities and approaches to work.

Be a role model for the type of connections you desire employees to build at work. Step forward and present yourself as a manager whom employees can trust. In everything you do, employees should feel like you are thinking about them and care about their sense of satisfaction at work. Even when there is conflict in a team, employees should feel like you are impartial and only seek the best outcomes for all parties involved.

Another way to demonstrate trust is to show employees recognition for their contributions. Don't keep quiet when you notice a team member stepping outside of their comfort zone, sacrificing their time for the team, or going above and beyond their duties. Even small acts of kindness around the office should be praised, especially if it's behavior that aligns with your values. Speaking up when employees are doing well feels gratifying and causes them to see the impact they are making on the company.

If you are on a mission to build trust, you can start by asking your team to fill out a questionnaire. Create a list of questions asking employees to rate their experience at the company and work closely with their manager. Don't ask for any names, emails, or other identifying information. Keeping the questionnaire anonymous will ensure you get honest feedback.

Leave a sealed box with a slot in the center in an accessible place around the office and ask employees to drop their completed sheets of paper in the box. If the questionnaire is online, send an email link to every employee that will guide them to the form.

Some of the questions you might ask employees include:

1. I believe the company is doing enough to support me with work tasks.
2. I feel comfortable approaching the manager with my concerns.
3. I know that if I work hard, I will be recognized and rewarded for my work.
4. I believe that I am treated fairly at work.
5. I feel safe raising objections about company policies and procedures.
6. I believe the company cares about my needs and personal well-being as an employee.

7. I believe I have my manager's undivided attention during conversation.
8. I have access to my manager whenever I need support from them.
9. I feel trusted by my manager to work on tasks without being micromanaged.
10. I believe that my manager is open to receiving constructive feedback from me.

Set a deadline for submissions of the forms, then gather and analyze the data. Go through the results as the management team before sitting down with employees and hosting an open discussion where they can bring up issues and together seek the best solutions.

O: Offering Support

The advantage of collaborative environments is that employees don't have to feel alone when they are working on tasks or going through various challenges. The presence of support allows them to manage stress better and prevent temporary mishaps from interfering with their performance.

Once again, as a leader, you will need to set the tone for the type of supportive environment you envision at work. Reinforce the habits you would like employees to adopt by setting expectations that the entire team (including you) are encouraged to strive toward.

Depending on your values and culture, some of these expectations can include:

- **Greetings and small talk.** Start and end each day with a friendly greeting and send-off. Encourage some small talk amongst employees about weekend plans or family updates. This helps the team get to know each other on a personal level and build a deeper level of trust and support.
- **Create a virtual support channel.** On your workplace communication app or platform, create a channel exclusively for venting, asking for help, or confiding in coworkers on a personal issue. Before launching the channel, establish a few rules about what type of content is allowed or prohibited. Offer alternative channels for discussing serious matters like workplace discrimination, harassment, and traumatic experiences.
- **Incentivize volunteering time.** To promote a culture of supportive teams, create attractive rewards for employees who volunteer their time to help colleagues. For example, you can make milestones based on the number of hours dedicated to helping others. Whenever employees reach a milestone, they get to select a

reward out of a list of meaningful items, such as money, gift cards,, concert tickets, dinner for two, all expenses paid meals, and so on.

- **Schedule regular team-building events.** Some teams need to leave the office and bond over experiences in order to strengthen their connection. Schedule regular team building events, where teams can spend the day completing an adventure, solving a creative problem, socializing at a restaurant, or giving back to charity. Pick an activity that incorporates common interests so that everyone walks away feeling positive about the experience.
- **Make positivity aspirational.** Support comes in different ways, such as offering time, service, or encouragement. You can promote positive reinforcement by making it "cool" to openly praise or compliment colleagues at work. For instance, you can find an empty wall in the office that you can convert into an appreciation wall. Cover the wall in chalk paint and leave a few pieces of chalk for employees to write down messages of support and gratitude to one another. You can also hang up photos of the "Employee of the Month" and other employees who have

recently achieved personal or professional achievements.

Creating a supportive culture is about being intentional about staying in touch with employees and keeping the conversation going between them. Implementing various inclusive work practices is a great way to show support without overdoing it.

R: Respect

You may already know the importance of mutual respect in fostering healthy team dynamics. In diverse teams, respect allows employees to tolerate each other's differences and maintain a professional environment.

Some employees confuse respect with being in agreement with how colleagues behave or choose to express themselves on the team. For example, two members of a team may experience a personality clash and assume they don't need to respect each other, however, this isn't what respect entails.

When you respect someone, you give them the level of understanding and consideration you would like to receive from others. You don't need to form a strong connection to give them the courtesy of feeling seen and heard. Respect is a fundamental right for every employee at work, regardless of how close or distant you may feel toward them. Employees should also understand that respecting each other is a standard requirement for collaboration and making sure everyone across structures and departments feels a sense of belonging at work.

To make respect an integral part of your company culture, consider creating policies about respectful behaviors at work; these may include conflict resolution policies, feedback policies, online and offline communication policies, and inclusion and representation policies. Make sure that everybody is aware of the behaviors expected at work by consistently bringing up policies during meetings and discussions.

Of course, employees will also be watching to see just how much you respect and honor these policies through your actions. Below are some of the respectful behaviors they will expect to see from you:

- **How well do you listen to employees?** The most basic sign of respect is listening to others when they are speaking. Being a good listener tells employees that you value their contributions and are willing to show support. It is never a good idea to have a conversation when you are busy or pressed for time.

Schedule meetings in advance to ensure you give employees your undivided attention.

- **How open are you to different opinions?** Another component of respect is tolerance. Instead of attempting to control the beliefs of employees or dictate how they should work or manage their time, you allow them to think and organize themselves in a way that feels comfortable to them. Employees want to know that raising concerns with you won't get them in trouble or ruin their reputation in the company.

- **How often do you praise efforts?** Showing appreciation is a sign of respect. When employees are recognized for their hard work, they feel valued by the company. You don't need to wait for big milestones to recognize the performance of your team. In fact, it can be more encouraging for them to receive praise for their progress rather than big accomplishments.

It is also important to show appreciation in different ways relevant to each occasion. For example, writing a personalized thank-you letter to a top-performing employee would be more appropriate than making a company-wide announcement. Lastly, feel free to ask employees how they desire to be recognized for their work. You may be surprised to find that monetary rewards rarely make it to the top of the list!

Bear in mind that there will be times when you or your team find it difficult to show respect. At the end of the day, we are all human beings, and our emotions can get the best of us. The worst thing to do when you aren't able to give respect is to engage in dialogue. This will only exacerbate interpersonal conflict. Take some time off and process how you are feeling and encourage employees to do the same. Once you feel more calm and regulated, you can begin to engage in conflict resolution.

A: Adaptability

Adaptability is the ability to change according to the demands of your environment. In the context of work, adaptability can be described as being responsive to changing needs and dynamics of teams.

It is difficult to respond to change when you or your team are inflexible, meaning you aren't open to learning new skills and practices that can help you solve problems and deepen your relationships. In other words, you prefer to stay in your comfort zone and continue leading your team the old-fashioned way.

The danger with this approach is that you miss out on the opportunity to capitalize on change. Yes, with change comes new possibilities that have the potential to positively impact your company and team dynamic.

A good example to illustrate this point is discrimination at work. Any form of discrimination requires urgent intervention since it violates the rights of employees. However, the way you choose to resolve this issue can be a test of how open you are to change.

There are two ways you can go about it: Undergo disciplinary action to respond to the violation, or undergo disciplinary action and take the opportunity to implement DEI initiatives that provide education about workplace inequality and how it impacts teams.

Both options would be appropriate, but the second option shows adaptability to change. Instead of fixing problems using safe methods, you can respond with new solutions that bring the team together and leave you better off than when you started.

There are many instances at work where employees would need to practice adaptability. Some of these include:

- When working across departments or with new team members, there could be a difference of opinion or a clash of communication styles. Being adaptable would help employees negotiate a way forward that makes everyone feel comfortable.

- When the company changes or makes updates to systems, employees may need to learn new processes. For employees who are resistant to change, the learning curve can be frustrating. Being adaptable can help them keep an open mind while getting accustomed to the new systems.

- When the business grows and employees are given more tasks to complete, being adaptable enables them to adjust their work schedule and find ways to maximize their time (i.e., assessing which tasks are urgent, important, or can be reassigned to someone else).

- When unexpected social or economic changes impact business growth, employees need to be prepared for uncomfortable changes to how they work. For example, they may forfeit their bonuses at the end of the year or must adopt a flexible work schedule.

Change in itself is not threatening. It is the fear of the unknown that makes employees resistant to stepping out of their comfort zones. If you would like to build a resilient team that stays together during uncomfortable moments, here are some practices you can reinforce at work:

- **Encourage asking questions and taking ownership of seeking answers.** When employees are confused about how to approach certain tasks, encourage them to ask questions and go on a search for answers. Step away as the manager and allow them to troubleshoot on their own.
- **Encourage employees to set their own weekly, monthly, and quarterly goals.** Doing this allows them to reflect on their own performance, set milestones that suit their own pace, and feel responsible for the outcomes.
- **Encourage employees to continuously work on their personal development.** You can get the whole office involved by starting a reading or fitness challenge, or create a mentorship and training programs where employees are taught various soft and technical skills.

Change is an inevitable part of every organization. The only way to get better results is to put yourself in uncomfortable situations and learn how to overcome those challenges. Make sure you recognize and reward teams or specific employees who demonstrate flexibility during difficult projects or company transitions.

T: Transparency

If you want to see more engagement in your team, then you may need to assess how transparent you are with communication. Statistics show that employees who feel there is enough transparency at work experience 12 times more job satisfaction than employees who feel there isn't enough transparency at work (Cooks-Campbell, 2022).

So, what is it about transparency that makes employees feel happier and more engaged at work? Transparency is a type of open communication between managers and employees. In traditional workplaces, there isn't much back-and-forth communication between managers and employees. The only time they engage is when instructions or feedback is given.

What makes transparency feel so rewarding is that employees feel trusted by their leaders. They are given an insider's look into the company, such as receiving updates on the growth of the company, challenges they are currently facing, and possible opportunities to exploit. This level of information sharing requires a great deal of trust, and thus employees feel honored to be treated with such high regard by their superiors.

When managers are so open and liberal with sharing information, it encourages employees to see themselves as more than just paid laborers. Instead, they see themselves as partners or collaborators who are valued stakeholders of the company. In turn, this positive mindset causes employees to take pride in their work and go above and beyond to achieve company goals.

Transparency and trust go hand in hand. Employees look to you as their leader to set expectations around communication. When you are closed off and measured in the way you communicate with your team, they may feel a disconnection from you, which affects how they feel about their jobs. But being open, approachable, and understanding makes it a lot easier for them to build relationships with you and have difficult conversations without fear of judgment.

For example, bringing up the topics of diversity, equity, and inclusion requires a safe space to share different views freely. If employees don't feel safe expressing their thoughts around each other or with their manager, then this will be an unproductive exercise. Thus, forming trust can lead to transparent communication, but initiating transparent communication is also a great way to build trust.

There are several practices that can help you create a transparent environment at work. These include:

Improve Your Recruitment and Onboarding Process

A job application is usually the first contact a potential employee has with your company. From the get-go, it is important to show transparency by being honest and upfront about the qualifying criteria, how much you are willing to pay and any benefits offered, the type of work schedule they will have, and so on.

When onboarding successful candidates, make sure you spend at least one week familiarizing them with the company, workplace, and policies or procedures they will need to follow. After the onboarding is complete, they should be clear about their job duties, who they report to, how to set up their emails, and operate the company's systems.

Employees should feel prepared for the journey ahead and comfortable with the company resources they have been given to make their experience at work more enjoyable.

Be Clear About Your Expectations

Every individual on your team should be able to explain what they do and how their job contributes to the success of the organization. However, even more than that, they should understand what "success" means for them and the team.

The only way employees would be able to have this much clarity about their roles is if there was an open line of communication between you and them. While group meetings are necessary, there is also a need for one-on-one discussions where you can sit with each person and review their progress or set new goals. Offering employees as much guidance as possible allows them to feel confident in making decisions, solving problems, and taking responsibility for their work.

Encourage Employees to Be Themselves

Another way to promote transparency at work is to encourage employees to speak their minds and bring their personalities to work. Of course, rude or disrespectful behavior is prohibited, but the humor, quirks, and interests that make each person unique should be celebrated in the workplace.

When employees feel relaxed and free to speak their minds, they can raise personal concerns or group challenges as they arise. This gives you enough time to respond to issues while they are still minor and can be resolved through honest feedback sessions. Moreover, when employees are given the platform to speak and be heard, they are more likely to participate in bringing positive transformation to the organization.

E: Empathy

We touched on empathy earlier in the book, but what we haven't discussed is how empathetic leadership fosters collaboration. We can define empathetic leadership as the ability to recognize and respond to the needs of employees.

Leaders who show this level of consideration for their employees create a safe space for issues to be brought to the table and addressed. Furthermore, marginalized employees, who face different types of work challenges, are not afraid to raise concerns and suggest solutions to create a more equitable environment. With this much care shown to employees, they are more likely to feel fulfilled with their jobs and comfortable working in diverse teams.

There are a couple of barriers that affect the level of empathy leaders are able to demonstrate at work. The first is a lack of genuine concern and understanding for employees. Not every leader has the patience and passion for people. Some are more interested in the business aspect of managing people and therefore aren't the best at building and nurturing relationships. These types of leaders often maintain emotional distance and have a clinical way of supervising the team and mediating disputes.

Another barrier to empathy is self-centeredness. Leaders who prioritize their own needs and comforts above the team's needs and comforts aren't able to show acceptance and understanding for others. They may be less tolerant of employees who think or communicate differently from them than those who behave identically to them.

In the long run, this could create a type of work environment where employees are afraid to openly disagree with their leader or where favoritism determines which employees are given more support and guidance.

If you are not sure how to start making empathy an integral part of your leadership, practice regularly asking employees, "How can I help?" This is a reassuring question that shows the lines of communication are always open. Getting the timing right when asking the question is crucial.

For example, when you catch an employee looking confused, frustrated, or uncomfortable, mention what you are noticing and ask the question. You might say, "I notice you look confused. How can I help?" or "You seem very uncomfortable. How can I help?"

Lastly, get into the habit of checking your own biases and hang-ups as a leader to ensure that you can accept employees for who they are, not who you wish they were. You can also practice networking with leaders from diverse backgrounds to learn about their experiences managing teams and how they maintain positive relationships with employees.

TEAM BUILDING EXERCISE

Fill a bag with random household items, ranging from small to medium-sized objects and accessories. Divide your team into two smaller groups and ask a representative from each group to close their eyes and grab two items from the bag. Challenge them to spend 30 minutes brainstorming how they combine the items to create and market a new product on the market. The purpose of the exercise is to get them to collectively solve a problem.

IN SUMMARY

Effective collaboration is about helping employees see the value in working together to reach common goals. It also requires you, as the leader, to model positive behaviors you would like to see practiced at work. By introducing your team to these 11 components of collaboration, you can improve the way they interact with each other and approach everyday work challenges.

CREATE THE DREAM

By failing to prepare, you are preparing to fail.

— BENJAMIN FRANKLIN

DO YOU HAVE A VISION OF THE TEAM YOU WANT?

If you want to incorporate DEI into your existing company culture, you will need to envision what they might look like in practice, what changes you would need to implement, as well as your strategy to get buy-in from your team.

It is often the case that when leaders set a vision for their workplace, they fail to consider how their vision might work on a practical level and how open employees might be to learning new norms. Remember, your vision is only as effective as how influential it is. After all, your employees are the ones who will bring that vision to life!

A word to keep at the back of your mind when crafting a new vision for your team is alignment. Alignment refers to being in agreement with something. Your vision must align with your existing company values. This helps to give your vision legitimacy and makes it easier for employees to resonate with.

Your job is to find commonalities between the type of team you would like to build and the values you stand for as a company. When getting buy-in from employees, convince them by explaining these commonalities and how this change will move the team in the right direction.

Bear in mind that sharing your vision is optional but full of advantages nonetheless. Certainly, implementing the vision may take longer due to seeking feedback from employees and making adjustments to incorporate their ideas. However, taking the long route allows employees to feel included in the change taking place within the organization. Some may even feel a sense of responsibility to maintain the new practices because they care about the outcomes.

The following sections will describe five components of setting and enforcing a new vision for your team. The components can be summarized under the acronym DREAM. You have the liberty to choose whether or not to include team members in the process of creating a new DREAM. As mentioned above, you are likely to see higher responsiveness when you invite employees to participate in bringing about this change.

D: Define Your Goals

Before deciding on what DEI initiatives you want to implement, the first step is setting the right goals. Having goals provides your team with a sense of direction and specific outcomes they will strive to achieve. It also helps you keep track of your progress along the way and assess if you are hitting or missing targets.

So, how do you define your goals? The tried and tested SMART goal-setting method will help you articulate what exactly you hope to achieve. Here is an overview of the five steps:

- **Specific:** In simple language, state what you want to achieve. Keep the statement clear and concise to avoid any double-meaning.

- **Measurable:** Identify a metric that can help you determine how close you are to achieving the goal. This could be a number, percentage, or tangible results you can hold yourself accountable to.
- **Achievable:** Read over what you have written down so far and assess if the goal is realistic. In other words, do you have the time, skills, knowledge, or support required to achieve this goal? Make adjustments as needed.
- **Relevant:** Think about the current state of your team and determine whether the goal you have set is relevant. Ask yourself what value reaching the goal could potentially bring.
- **Time-bound:** Set a reasonable amount of time to achieve the goal. Bear in mind that your DEI initiatives will most likely be carried out in addition to your team's current workload. They could also fall outside of work hours (e.g., team building activities) and therefore need to be scheduled out.

If you decide to jointly define DEI goals with your team, be transparent about what types of goals you have already been thinking about. Share research or insights you have gathered over the past weeks or months that highlight the kinds of challenges your team is facing.

Of course, your team may already know about some of the challenges, like a recent case of discrimination. However, hearing about them and being given an opportunity to provide feedback makes the process of goal-setting feel more significant.

Below are ideas of meaningful goals to set with your team:

- To create monthly social events that educate the team on diverse cultures that are represented in the workplace.
- To organize quarterly diversity and inclusion training programs.
- To increase positive perceptions about teamwork by 30% in the first quarter in order to improve peer relationships.
- To invite one speaker bi-monthly to address the team on topics related to DEI.
- To establish a peer review program that allows employees to nominate a helpful and friendly colleague for a monthly cash bonus.

R: Reach Out to Marginalized Groups

Now that you have set your goals, it is time to identify and reach out to marginalized employees. You may know of a few on your team, but since they are less likely to speak out, there could be some that you haven't had a one-on-one conversation with.

You may be wondering why this step is necessary if the whole team is working toward making positive changes. Why isolate some and personally reach out? The answer boils down to power and rank. Since marginalized employees feel a sense of inferiority compared to other employees, they don't feel empowered to take part in group discussions or company initiatives. They may have negative perceptions of management, which cause them to keep their distance.

Reaching out to them on a one-on-one level is symbolic of extending an olive branch and showing how much you care about their sense of belonging at work. Moreover, the fact that someone higher up is reaching down and offering support can make marginalized employees feel the same kind of respect and appreciation every other employee feels on a regular basis.

Moving forward, you can also reach out to marginalized employees through the recruitment process. Just imagine how much confidence minority groups would feel stepping into a workplace that has already made preparations for them. Or one that already promotes diversity and inclusion. The type of engagement you would receive from them would be higher than if you hadn't made these considerations.

There are various ways you can implement diversity in recruiting and set minority groups up for success from the beginning. A few strategies include:

- **Improve your job ads.** Find ways to incorporate inclusive language in your job ads. Be mindful of unconscious bias, such as using "he" or "she" when describing a candidate instead of "they." Moreover, be careful not to use language that would be associated with a specific social class or persons of a particular age.
- **Post job ads on diverse platforms.** To make your job ads more accessible to a wide range of candidates, post them on platforms that are widely accessible. For example, opt for platforms that are popular across demographics and free for job seekers to browse and apply for jobs.
- **Offer educational training or internship programs to marginalized job seekers.** Another way to encourage more diversity at

work is to implement educational assistance programs for upcoming talent from underrepresented groups. These could be college graduates in their final year who are looking for summer work or mentorship programs. Find ways to make the program sustainable, such as hiring them afterward or helping them find jobs.

- **Implement blind resume screening.** One of the ways to reduce unconscious bias during the recruitment process is using blind resume screening. While sorting through the resumes, the recruiter or assistant will "black out" any identifying details about the candidate's age, gender, race, nationality, residential address, and so on. This enables the recruiter to have an objective and unbiased assessment of whether the candidate meets the requirements of the job.

Lastly, empowering marginalized employees is also about helping them realize that although they may sometimes feel powerless at work, they have choices. For example, they can choose which career path to take, how much time and effort to dedicate to their career goals, what type of mindset to adopt at work, and how much time and effort they dedicate to relationship building. To assist them in making empowered choices, reassess your policies and cultural practices at work to remove as many discriminatory barriers as possible.

E: Engage All Team Members

After you have reached out to marginalized employees, it is time to bring the whole team together and engage in meaningful discussions relevant to the goals you have set. It is common for team members to have questions or comments regarding the change you are embarking on. You can set the tone for the type of engagements you will be having in the future by approaching questions and comments with openness, empathy, and transparency.

In general, team members should be allowed to voice concerns or disagree at any point during discussions. Your level of empathy can effectively calm their fears and cause them to feel heard, even if the final decisions you make still stand.

Choose to see disagreements as opportunities to get to know employees better and learn about their perspectives. They bring a wealth of skills and experience to the team, which could assist in achieving shared goals. Be open to hearing their opinions without judgment and making enhancements to your goals or objectives.

One of the strategies companies use to keep teams engaged is to create employee resource groups (ERGs). As mentioned earlier in the book, these groups are created to bring like-minded people together and establish internal communities.

Belonging to an ERG allows employees and members to build connections across teams and departments with people who share similar identities and interests. If they are unable to feel a sense of belonging within their assigned team, they are at least given a chance to develop a community with other employees at the company.

In other words, having ERG takes away the stress or anxiety of not fitting in. Every employee can feel accepted at work by finding their smaller tribe. This initiative can strengthen collaboration within teams and cause greater fairness and tolerance across groups.

A: Address biases and barriers

It is important to think about the possible barriers that might get in the way of accomplishing your DEI goals. As good as your intentions may be, there are challenges like unconscious bias that can interfere with the work you are doing to bring your team together.

It is usually not enough to promote diversity and representation without being proactive about addressing workplace inequality. Plus, to get marginalized groups to buy into DEI initiatives, they will first need to see how much priority you place on creating a safe and equitable workplace.

Some of the ways to combat inequality at work include:

- **Understand what unconscious bias looks and sounds like.** One of the best ways to fight against inequality at work is to educate yourself on the various ways it can manifest and the underlying causes that might perpetuate it. Challenge yourself to spot examples of unconscious bias among employees or when reading real-life case studies of other companies. The more aware you are of unconscious bias, the quicker you can respond.
- **Get into the habit of questioning your thoughts.** Recognize that you are human and can sometimes analyze situations from a subjective point of view. Or maybe, at times, your decisions can unintentionally make certain groups of employees feel left out. It can be helpful to get into the habit of questioning your thoughts, so you can take a step back and assess if what you are thinking is fair. A few questions to ask yourself include:
- Are my thoughts based on facts or opinions?

- Could this be an emotionally-charged decision?
  Do I feel emotionally triggered?
- Are my thoughts playing at the extremes, such
  as being black or white?
- Are my thoughts generalizations made from
  past patterns and information?
- How would one of the leaders I admire make
  sense of this situation?
- **Use empathetic dialogue.** Another way to
  combat inequality at work is to learn how to
  confront emotional issues rather than allowing
  them to build up. These types of conversations
  are never easy due to how sensitive the topics
  may be, but they enable honest and transparent
  communication, which strengthens work
  relationships.

Difficult conversations require a great deal of understanding. Instead of seeking to be right, your aim is to
make the other person feel seen and heard. Empathetic
dialogue can help you manage difficult conversations
around inequality without jeopardizing the bonds you
have formed with employees.

There are three phrases to remember when having
empathetic dialogue:

- **Acknowledge the other person's experience.** Show the employee that you understand or at least can imagine what they are going through. Use validating phrases like, "I understand how upset you must feel."
- **Seek clarity to avoid misunderstandings.** It is important to understand the employee's full message before attempting to solve the problem or share your thoughts. A simple question to ask may be, "What I hear you saying is... would that be correct?"
- **Express the desire to solve the problem together.** The last thing you want is for an employee to feel alone after facing any kind of mistreatment at work. When you are ready to discuss a way forward, express your desire to help them address the issue, seek justice, or improve their working conditions. You might say, "I care about your sense of fulfillment at work and will do my best to help you resolve this matter."

In the long term, you can combat biases and other barriers by setting up a diversity and inclusion training program. The purpose of this program is to address existing interpersonal issues and educate employees on the importance of inclusion and representation in the workplace. The program can also teach employees crucial conflict resolution and communication skills that can enhance the quality of teamwork.

To create effective diversity and inclusion, extend the invitation to all staff and explore different types of issues that may be faced in diverse teams. Your program should also be aligned with your company's vision, mission, and values to help employees understand its significance.

Lastly, you should think about how to make your program sustainable in the long term. In general, successful programs run for many years and become an integral part of a company's culture.

Some of the ways to make your program sustainable are to provide free training, offer incentives for attending events, or incorporate DEI awareness in many of your work processes, such as recruitment and onboarding, human resource management, customer service, and so on. The aim is to ensure employees regularly participate in DEI initiatives taking place within your company.

M: Measure Progress and Success

One of the common reasons why DEI initiatives fail shortly after implementation is due to the lack of accountability around the programs. Leaders have the right ideas but overlook the importance of tracking and measurement tools. As such, they end up gathering a lot of data but don't know what to do with it or how to improve the impact of their programs.

Without the proper framework to build and monitor DEI initiatives, you won't be able to define and measure success. For example, your goal may be to hire diverse talent, but how many employees are searching for? What demographics should they come from? And what positions do you want them to fill in the company?

Having the right DEI metrics takes away a lot of the guesswork in implementing changes to your team. It also helps you assess if you are doing enough to promote diversity and inclusion or whether to double down on your efforts.

There are different metrics to use when measuring the effectiveness of your DEI initiatives. Some of them include:

- **Diversity of employees compared to the diversity of the application pool.** If your goal is to diversify your team at work, look at the types of people who are applying for jobs in your company compared to the people you end up hiring. In other words, if you took a sample of the people you hired, would it represent the diversity of the application pool? Or would it represent a minority?

- **Number of diverse employees across hierarchical structures.** While it is commendable to hire diverse talent, it is important to ensure marginalized people are represented across the organizational structures. For example, we know that women are still largely underrepresented in leadership positions. Creating programs that specifically offer leadership training and skills development to women can set them up for success and promotion within the company.

- **Percentage of job retention and satisfaction.** Another useful metric to measure DEI efforts is the level of job retention and satisfaction in your team. If employees feel satisfied and comfortable at work, they won't consider leaving. You can measure the job retention rate by taking the number of employees who left within a specific period and dividing that figure by the number of employees who worked in the company at the start of the period. Multiply the total by 100 and you will get the job retention rate. The formula can also be used to calculate which demographics are frequently leaving the company.

There is no standard when applying metrics. Read over your goals and find the most suitable measurement to determine success. You will also need to decide if your metrics are specific to marginalized workers or take the whole team into consideration. Some of the research tools you can use to collect the right information are:

- **Pre-employment assessment tools.** Before taking candidates through the interview process, you can blindly assess them to figure out if they are a good fit for the company. Pre-employment assessment tools collect information, such as a candidate's personality traits, strengths and weaknesses, emotional intelligence, leadership qualities, and so on. The data collected can help you filter out candidates who may not represent your company values and team culture.
- **Diversity and inclusion analytical tools.** There is software available to small and large businesses that can help you continually collect and analyze diversity and inclusion data. The insights gathered can help improve policies, improve recruitment processes, or plan effective skills development programs.
- **Company surveys.** If you want to collect employee feedback, you can create and

distribute online surveys. The survey can ask a series of short and long-form questions related to specific topics. Surveys are free and easy to customize. They can also be set to anonymous, which allows employees to freely express their opinions without fear of backlash.

Measuring the success of DEI initiatives is about collecting relevant data that can be used to bring about positive change in your team. However, without using the right metrics, the data collected would be meaningless. Therefore, take time to plan what you are going to measure and the best ways to measure it.

TEAM BUILDING EXERCISE

Organize a day trip to a local charity or shelter where your team can volunteer. The purpose of the trip is to bring the team together to assist with a noble cause. Allow the team to decide among themselves what tasks they will each be responsible for on the day and how they will measure the success of the project.

IN SUMMARY

Bringing transformation within your team is possible; however, there must be a clear vision to guide your efforts. Once you have decided on the vision, share it with your team and get them excited about being part of the change. The five-step DREAM process can help you stay organized when planning and executing DEI initiatives while encouraging all employees to get involved.

ASSESS AND DO IT ALL OVER AGAIN

We need to reach that happy stage of our development when differences and diversity are not seen as sources of division and distrust, but of strength and inspiration.

— JOSEFA ILOILO

ASSESS YOUR COMPANY POLICIES

A common mistake that leaders make is to sit back and wait for the company culture to form organically. They overlook the need to define the philosophy at work, describe acceptable behaviors, and set expectations of how employees should interact with one another.

A few problems arise because of this, namely, people are hired without being vetted for alignment with the team expectations, generic policies are adopted that do not match the dynamic of the team, and managers aren't trained to become empathetic leaders who communicate effectively and create an environment that allows employees to express themselves.

The whole idea of letting the culture form organically can threaten the unity of teams and, even worst-case scenarios, lead to disengagement and high turnover. Since this isn't something that you want to see happening at work, it is good to continually evaluate and define your company culture and see whether your policies and procedures represent the diverse talent of people who work for you.

The first step to evaluating policies and procedures is to go back and read them. You would be surprised at how many leaders participate in creating company documents once and never review them again. Documents like work policies are the framework that determines the health of your office life. As the company evolves, these policies need to be updated to match the renewed vision and goals of work life.

Every policy ought to have a strong purpose behind it; otherwise, it may not be a relevant policy to have. By just looking at the name of the policy, you should be able to tell what it is about, as well as what value it promises to add to your work life. Read the policy and determine how frequently it is referred to and followed at work.

Think of all the employees it would affect and if there are any people who are exempt from the rule. This level of analysis should help you decipher how effective the policy is currently in your workplace and whether it needs to be removed or revised.

You can also evaluate your policies in light of the modern workplace challenges companies face, such as a lack of diversity, equity, and inclusion. Ask yourself whether your policies are relevant enough to address these issues and protect the interests of all employees. For example, do your policies about attire at work represent the interests of employees who are gender fluid, or do they assume that a man wears suits and a woman wears dresses?

If you are not clued up about the nuances of diversity and representation, it might help to sit down with a DEI expert when revising your company policies. They may be able to pick up on phrases or language that involves biases and offer inclusive alternatives.

HOW TO CREATE INCLUSIVE POLICIES

You cannot seek to improve team dynamics without making updates to your policies. In most cases, when you need to hold employees accountable, you will refer them to the company policies. Imagine how embarrassing it would be to implement disciplinary hearings about workplace discrimination and refer to outdated policies that don't list or mention anything about the form of discrimination you are addressing.

Or think about the legal trouble you would incur if a frustrated employee highlighted a company policy that infringes on their rights. You can avoid these problems by regularly evaluating and revising your policies to enforce better accountability at work and reflect the interests of your diverse team.

There are five steps you can follow to create inclusive policies, which are:

Study Past and Current Policies and Procedures

Dedicate a few days to studying your company handbooks and noting down all of your policies and procedures. Read through them and highlight any "red flags" or things that you would like another manager to give feedback on.

Read Up On What Other Companies Are Doing

Do some research on DEI policies that companies have implemented, which have been successful in retaining the best talent. Bear in mind that your company culture may be different, and the same policy may not work identically in your team. The purpose of this exercise is to get inspiration by seeing what policies are already out there and how you might customize them for your workplace.

Interview Employees

When creating or updating policies, the leadership tends to meet alone and discuss what needs to be changed. Rarely will you find leaders engaging with employees to find out what type of policies and procedures they would like to see.

Of course, there is a risk to opening the floor for dialogue on policies. Some employees may see it as an excuse to speak negatively about the company or criticize ideas that are brought up by others.

To mitigate the risk of counterproductive discussions, schedule one-on-one interviews with every employee at work. Not only will this extra effort make them feel valued, but it will also allow them to speak freely away from colleagues. Ask various questions related to past, current, and future policies they would like to see.

Formulate and Test New Policies

After gathering the necessary data, you can meet the leadership team and formulate the new or revised policies. These meetings can be private and confidential.

Note that there will be a lot of back-and-forth debating among the leaders of the company about how to structure or implement various policies. If you cannot reach an agreement, it can be useful to have a third-party DEI expert or consultant who can help you formulate policies.

Once that job is done, you can introduce the new policies to the team, but emphasize that you are still in the testing phase. The testing phase is when policies are adopted temporarily and reviewed by managers and employees to see how well they work.

During this phase, employees may be asked to take surveys or attend DEI training programs. The aim is to prepare the team for the new journey they are about to embark on and address any concerns or issues that may arise.

Formally Announce Policies and Update Company Documents

When the testing phase is complete, and you have made the final revisions and consulted with the relevant stakeholders, it is time to formally announce the new policies and update company documents.

The first announcement should be made to the people most affected by the policies—your team. The preferred method is a face-to-face meeting followed by a company-wide email broadcast. It is important to state that feedback on the new policies is still welcome and can be offered through the right communication channels.

The second announcement can be made to other stakeholders, like investors, customers, and vendors. This announcement can be made over an email, company website, or social media post. Feedback isn't necessary when addressing external stakeholders; however, you can take note of the comments made.

Lastly, remember to update your company documents to reflect the changes made to your policies. For example, you will need to update your recruitment guidelines, payroll policies, company application forms, code of conduct, and any other related resources.

Continue to monitor your team and general interactions at work. Keep the lines of communication open so that employees can raise questions or give feedback whenever they run into challenges. You can also keep the DEI training program running so that employees have access to education about diversity and inclusion.

TEAM BUILDING EXERCISE

Host a panel discussion with DEI experts and coaches, virtually or at the office. Invite your team to attend the event and bring along prepared questions. The aim is to expose your team to different perspectives about diversity and inclusion from people who work closely with companies to facilitate training programs.

IN SUMMARY

When you are getting ready to implement change in your team, make sure you make the necessary revisions to your company policies. Since these policies create the framework for your workplace, they must reflect the updates you have made to your culture. When creating or revising policies, don't hesitate to consult with trained DEI experts who can help you through the process.

Before You Go...

If this book has inspired you to put the "Three Cs" into action, it would be awesome if you could leave a review on Amazon.

Share what you liked about it and a little bit about your own story. Help other readers see an openness to change as the first step towards building a truly diverse, equitable, inclusive company culture.

LEAVE A REVIEW!

Thank you for your support. Your commitment to achieving progress through a visionary, impactful, employee-centered DEI policy will make top candidates want to work for you...and keep working for you. Allow other managers to know that they can change lives and achieve unprecedented success while they're at it.

Scan the QR code below

CONCLUSION

You have a responsibility to make inclusion a daily thought, so we can get rid of the word "inclusion."

— THEODORE MELFI

Once a year, a few companies around the world are rated the "Best Place to Work" by industry magazines. These companies tend to score high on employee engagement and satisfaction. Some of the words employees from these companies use to describe their place of work are "dream job," "friendly atmosphere," and "safe community."

Any leader who is passionate about their company will undoubtedly care about the experience of employees at work. They understand how employee-related challenges impact performance and the bottom line. Moreover, they see the long-term effects of dysfunctional team dynamics on the overall culture at work. Thus, they conclude that unhappy employees lead to bad business.

The main themes explored in this book have been diversity, equity, and inclusion. These are factors that are fundamental for employees to feel a sense of belonging and acceptance at work. The reason DEI is such an important area to focus on is because a lack of DEI perpetuates inequalities and discrimination at work.

Certainly, all employees are equal despite their race, gender, nationality, religion, or sexuality. However, equality is not the same as equity. To prevent social inequalities from manifesting at work, companies must look at how they can make their teams, policies, and overall culture more inclusive of marginalized groups of workers. On a practical level, this could involve revising income structures, using inclusive language, hiring competent people of color into leadership positions, and implementing DEI programs.

If you are in the process of making your company the "Best Place to Work," then you will find this book helpful. By practicing the 3 C's—Communicate, Collaborate, and Create—you will learn how to structure your team so everybody feels valued regardless of their differences. Every member of your team will feel respected, even when they have disagreements with each other because what matters most to them is maintaining a space where difficult conversations are brought up and solutions discussed without compromising trust.

If reading this book has helped you positively transform your team, please leave a review on Amazon!

GLOSSARY

Collaboration: The act of working together with others to solve problems and produce something meaningful.

DEI policies: Company principles that promote representation and participation of marginalized employees.

DEI programs: Company initiatives that promote representation and participation of marginalized employees.

Diversity: The coming together of people from different socioeconomic backgrounds.

Discrimination: Unfair and negative treatment of people based on personal attributes, such as their age, race, gender, religion, or sexuality.

Emotional intelligence: The ability to understand and recognize your emotions and the emotional experiences of others.

Empathy: The ability to immerse yourself into another person's world and understand how they perceive reality.

Equity: Understanding the different challenges faced by employees and offering support that affords everyone equal access to opportunities.

Inclusion: Making everyone feel seen and heard at work.

Marginalized groups: Employees who come from underrepresented communities in society based on race, gender, ethnicity, sexuality, and religion.

Minority groups: See "marginalized groups."

Microaggression: Indirect negative attitudes and behaviors, or unintentional discrimination, directed at marginalized groups.

Privileged groups: Employees that are given certain benefits, protection, and unearned advantages in society and at work by virtue of belonging to a particular race, ethnicity, gender, or religion.

Representation: The feeling of being included and supported within a group.

Self-awareness: The ability to understand and recognize your thoughts and feelings.

Self-regulation: The ability to control and monitor your thoughts and feelings.

Social inequality: Injustices that affect certain people in society, which limits their access to services, resources, power, social status, and certain lifestyle choices.

Unconscious bias: Negative attitudes, assumptions, or stereotypes that are held, which affect how you think or feel about certain people.

REFERENCES

Admin. (2019, February 1). *Workplace culture: What it is, why it matters, and how to define it.* Your Erc. https://yourerc.com/blog/post/work place-culture-what-it-is-why-it-matters-how-to-define-it

Asana. (2022, November 18). *Collaboration in the workplace: 11 Ways to boost performance.* Asana. https://asana.com/resources/collabora tion-in-the-workplace

Baragwanath, T. (n.d.). *Why workplace collaboration is the secret sauce to higher retention and better business outcomes.* 360Learning. https://360learning.com/blog/why-is-collaboration-important/

Baumgartner, N. (2022, June 22). *Creating an inclusive culture: Five actionable ways leaders can foster a greater sense of belonging.* Forbes. https://www.forbes.com/sites/forbeshumanresourcescouncil/2022/06/22/creating-an-inclusive-culture-five-actionable-ways-leaders-can-foster-a-greater-sense-of-belonging/?sh=7bff02803d8d

Bilanich, B. (2009, July 5). *Sincerity, clear language and success.* Fast Company. https://www.fastcompany.com/1278844/sincerity-clear-language-and-success#:~:text=Sincerity%20enhances%20communication

Bit.AI. (2018, June 14). *21 Collaboration statistics that show the power of teamwork.* Bit Blog; Blog.Bit.ai. https://blog.bit.ai/collaboration-statistics/

Brearley, B. (2017, March 21). *5 Powerful ways to create open communication in your team.* Thoughtful Leader. https://www.thoughtfulleader.com/encouraging-open-communication/

Chally Library. (2022, February 21). *56 Inspirational diversity and inclusion quotes for the workplace.* Chally. https://chally.com/blog/inclu sion-quotes/#:~:text=%E2%80%9CI%20can%20tell%20you%2C%20without

Chally. (2022, February 21). *56 Inspirational Diversity And Inclusion*

Quotes For The Workplace. https://chally.com/blog/inclusion-quotes/

Cherry, K. (2022, January 26). *5 Key components of emotional intelligence.* Verywell Mind. https://www.verywellmind.com/components-of-emotional-intelligence-2795438

Conley, M. (2018). *45 Quotes that celebrate teamwork, hard work, and collaboration.* Hubspot. https://blog.hubspot.com/marketing/team work-quotes

Cooks-Campbell, A. (2022, August 29). *Transparency in the workplace: What it is (and what to avoid).* Better Up. https://www.betterup.com/blog/transparency-in-the-workplace

Cooney, C. (2021, May 7). *55% of people are too scared to talk about diversity and inclusion in the workplace for fear of saying the wrong thing.* RightTrack Learning. https://righttracklearning.com/fear-of-saying-wrong-thing-at-work/

Crookes, L. (2021, September 7). *What's in a name? Addressing name bias in recruitment.* LinkedIn. https://www.linkedin.com/pulse/whats-name-addressing-bias-recruitment-lucy-crookes/

Culture Vulture. (n.d.). *3 Real-life examples of cultural misunderstandings in business.* Commisceo Global Consulting Ltd. https://www.commisceo-global.com/blog/3-real-life-examples-of-cultural-misunderstandings-in-business#:~:text=You%20don

deBara, D. (2023, February 24). *The different types of workplace discrimination (with examples).* Hourly. https://www.hourly.io/post/work place-discrimination

Diversus Health. (2021, April 30). *How to have honest conversations.* Diversus Health. https://diversushealth.org/how-to-have-honest-conversations/

Dutta, D. (2020, February 20). *25 Powerful diversity and inclusion quotes for a stronger company culture.* Vantage Circle HR Blog. https://blog.vantagecircle.com/diversity-and-inclusion-quotes/

Easy Llama. (n.d.). *How does unconscious bias affect the workplace? Everything you need to know.* Easy Llama. https://www.easyllama.com/blog/how-does-unconscious-bias-affect-the-workplace/#:~:text=When%20unconscious%20bias%20is%20not

Economic Policy Institute. (2021). *Current population survey extracts*. EPI Microdata Extracts. https://microdata.epi.org/

Erica. (2021, February 25). *Diversity and inclusion metrics: What and how to measure*. Harver. https://harver.com/blog/diversity-inclusion-metrics/

Fallon, N. (2023, February 21). *How to create an inclusive workplace culture*. Business News Daily. https://www.businessnewsdaily.com/10055-create-inclusive-workplace-culture.html

Franklin, B. (2019). *Benjamin Franklin quote*. Brainy Quote; Brainy-Quote. https://www.brainyquote.com/quotes/benjamin_franklin_138217

Garfinkle, J. (2019). *7 Steps to clear and effective communication*. Garfinkle Executive Coaching. https://garfinkleexecutivecoaching.com/articles/improve-your-communication-skills/seven-steps-to-clear-and-effective-communication

Get Impactly. (n.d.). *Why is empathy important in the workplace: 4 Benefits at the workplace*. Get Impactly. https://www.getimpactly.com/post/empathy-important-in-the-workplace

Gitnux. (2023a, February 22). *Racism in the workplace statistics 2023: Key insights and trends*. Gitnux. https://blog.gitnux.com/racism-in-the-workplace-statistics/

Gitnux. (2023b, March 23). *The most surprising gender inequality workplace statistics and trends in 2023*. Gitnux. https://blog.gitnux.com/gender-inequality-workplace-statistics/

Gould, E., & Kassa, M. (2021, May 20). *Low-wage, low-hours workers were hit hardest in the COVID-19 recession: The State of Working America 2020 employment report*. Economic Policy Institute. https://www.epi.org/publication/swa-2020-employment-report/

Griffin, T. (2021, February 7). *How to communicate effectively (in any situation)*. Thomas Griffin. https://thomasgriffin.com/how-to-communicate-effectively/

Grossman, D. (2019, May 6). *Trust in the workplace: 6 Steps to building trust with employees*. Your Thought Partner. https://www.yourthoughtpartner.com/blog/bid/59619/leaders-follow-these-6-steps-to-build-trust-with-employees-improve-how-you-re-perceived

Hari, V. (2020, December 31). *Workplace bias and its impact on organizations.* CecureUs. https://cecureus.com/workplace-bias-and-its-impact-on-organizations/

Hawley, M. (2023, February 28). *Unpacking DEI training: How to measure its real impact.* Reworked.co. https://www.reworked.co/employee-experience/most-dei-training-doesnt-work-heres-how-to-tie-training-to-impact/#:~:text=Researchers%20have%20studied%20the%20effects

He, G. (2022, May 8). *Diversity and inclusion activities and ideas for the office in 2022.* Team Building. https://teambuilding.com/blog/diversity-and-inclusion-activities

Henderson, T. (2020, September 28). *Mothers are 3 times more likely than fathers to have lost jobs in pandemic.* Stateline. https://stateline.org/2020/09/28/mothers-are-3-times-more-likely-than-fathers-to-have-lost-jobs-in-pandemic/

Ideas Fest. (2023, January 3). *Why does representation matter in the workplace?* Fresh Business Thinking. https://www.freshbusinessthinking.com/latest/why-does-representation-matter-in-the-workplace/51229.article

In Professional Development. (2022, April 1). *3 Ways emotional intelligence will improve your communication.* INPD. https://www.inpd.co.uk/blog/3-ways-emotional-intelligence-will-improve-your-communication

Inclusive Employers. (2022, June 14). *What is inclusive language?* Inclusive Employers. https://www.inclusiveemployers.co.uk/blog/what-is-inclusive-language-how-to-use-it-in-the-workplace/?cn-reloaded=1&cn-reloaded=1

Indeed Editorial Team. (2022, June 25). *56 Inspiring team communication quotes to motivate your team.* Indeed Career Guide. https://www.indeed.com/career-advice/career-development/team-communication-quotes

Indeed Editorial Team. (2023a, February 4). *How to effectively use active listening in the workplace.* Indeed Career Guide. https://www.indeed.com/career-advice/career-development/listening-in-the-workplace

Indeed Editorial Team. (2023b, February 28). *9 Ways to help and support colleagues at work.* Indeed. https://www.indeed.com/career-advice/career-development/helping-and-supporting-others-at-work#:~:text=Helping%20your%20colleagues%20at%20work,more%20likely%20to%20support%20you

International Labour Office. (2021). *Inequalities and the world of work.* International Labour Office. https://www.ilo.org/wcmsp5/groups/public/---ed_norm/---relconf/documents/meetingdocument/wcms_792123.pdf

Jackson, D. (2017, December 28). *Why your employees hate collaborating – and how you can fix it.* Entrepreneur Resources. https://www.entrepreneur-resources.net/employees-hate-collaborating-can-fix

Johansson, E. (2021, July 2). *Big tech diversity: Google's losing minority employees fast.* Verdict. https://www.verdict.co.uk/google-diversity/

Khan, H. (2021, April 19). *The causes and effects of poor communication in the workplace.* Simpplr. https://www.simpplr.com/blog/2021/causes-effects-poor-communication-workplace/

Klein, M. (2022, March 10). *The importance of open communication in the workplace.* Blink. https://joinblink.com/intelligence/open-communication-importance/

Korn Ferry. (n.d.). *6 Ways to empower underrepresented groups in the workplace.* Korn Ferry. https://www.kornferry.com/insights/featured-topics/diversity-equity-inclusion/empower-underrepresented-groups-in-the-workplace

Lemzy, A. (n.d.). *5 Reasons diversity and inclusion initiatives are challenging.* Delivering Happiness. https://blog.deliveringhappiness.com/5-reasons-diversity-inclusion-initiatives-are-challenging#:~:text=Differing%20Perspectives

Lencioni, P. (2002). *The five dysfunctions of a team : a leadership fable.* Jossey-Bass.

Long, B. (2022, October 12). *Transparency in the workplace: Everything you need to know.* Insight Global. https://insightglobal.com/blog/transparency-in-the-workplace/

Markovic, I. (2023). *Why giving instant feedback is important for effective learning*. Edume. https://www.edume.com/blog/role-of-feedback-in-improving-learning#:~:text=It

Martic, K. (2020, June 23). *Trust in the workplace: Why it Is so important today and how to build it*. Haiilo. https://haiilo.com/blog/trust-in-the-workplace-why-it-is-so-important-today-and-how-to-build-it/

Mayo Clinic. (2020, May 29). *Stressed out? Be assertive*. Mayo Clinic. https://www.mayoclinic.org/healthy-lifestyle/stress-management/in-depth/assertive/art-20044644

Mcconnell, B. (2021, July 30). *12 Ways to improve your diversity recruiting strategy*. Recruitee. https://recruitee.com/articles/diversity-recruiting-strategy

Mendez, J. (2017, April 27). *The impact of biases and how to prevent their interference in the workplace*. Insight into Diversity. https://www.insightintodiversity.com/the-impact-of-biases-and-how-to-prevent-their-interference-in-the-workplace/

Morgan, N. (n.d.). *11 Steps to creating a shared vision for your team*. Ellevate Network. https://www.ellevatenetwork.com/articles/7542-11-steps-to-creating-a-shared-vision-for-your-team

O'Reilly. (n.d.). 44. *Understanding and overcoming the five dysfunctions*. Oreilly. https://www.oreilly.com/library/view/the-five-dysfunctions/9780787960759/ch44.html#suggestions_for_overcoming_dysfunction_i

Parks, L. (2022, April 29). *Why representation matters in the workplace*. The Nova Collective. https://thenovacollective.com/why-representation-matters-in-the-workplace/#:~:text=With%20a%20wide%20variety%20of

Plesco, L. (2016, June 30). *7 Ways "PROMPT" communication provokes a response on-camera, on-stage and online*. LinkedIn. https://www.linkedin.com/pulse/7-ways-use-prompt-communication-lauri-plesco/

Quantive. (n.d.). *8 DEI challenges leaders face (and how to solve them)*. Quantive. https://quantive.com/resources/articles/dei-challenges

Rai, T., & Dutkiewicz, C. (2022, May 10). *DEI efforts: How to deal with pushback and obstacles*. Gartner. https://www.gartner.com/en/arti

cles/how-to-navigate-pushback-to-diversity-equity-and-inclusion-efforts

Ray, S. A. (n.d.). *Sri Amit Ray quotes (author of Power of Exponential Mindset for Success and Leadership)*. Goodreads. https://www. goodreads.com/author/quotes/22787958.Sri_Amit_Ray#:~:text=% E2%80%9CIf%20you%20do%20not%20lead

Re-edition. (n.d.). *How to evaluate policies and procedures*. Reedition Magazine. https://www.reeditionmagazine.com/to-the-minute/ how-to-evaluate-policies-and-procedures

Reiners, B. (2023, March 28). *50 Diversity In The Workplace Statistics To Know*. Built In. https://builtin.com/diversity-inclusion/diversity-in-the-workplace-statistics

Sayon, E. (2023, June 1). *Effects of ineffective communication in the workplace*. Public Spectrum. https://publicspectrum.co/effects-of-ineffec tive-communication-in-the-workplace/

Shoobridge, G. (2020, January 6). *Does the "golden rule" still hold up in our modern workplace?* LinkedIn. https://www.linkedin.com/pulse/ does-golden-rule-still-hold-up-our-modern-workplace-gonzalo

Spalding, T. (2011, June 16). *Rank: How power and privilege affect our relationships*. Knockalla. http://www.knockalla.net/rank-how-power-and-privilege-affect-our-relationships/

Srinivasan , R. (2021, March 19). *A culture that lacks inclusion hurts everyone*. The University of Texas at Austin News. https://news.utexas. edu/2021/03/19/a-culture-that-lacks-inclusion-hurts-everyone/#: ~:text=A%20lack%20of%20inclusion%20in

Sylvan, R. (2017, September 26). *Example of manual policies and procedures*. Bizfluent. https://bizfluent.com/about-5821769-example-manual-policies-procedures.html

Tsang, S. (2020, June 25). *3 Ways to promote accountability in the workplace*. Fond. https://www.fond.co/blog/accountability-in-the-workplace/

Ugwu, C. (n.d.). *25 Effective diversity team building activities in 2022*. Gomada. https://www.gomada.co/blog/diversity-team-building-activities

Uzialko, A. (2022, June 29). *If you listen up, your employees will step up*.

Business News Daily. https://www.businessnewsdaily.com/1934-leadership-listening-employee-input-initiative.html

Wauls, D. (2021, May 4). *Respectful communication at work.* Samaritan Center. https://samaritanlancaster.org/blog/how-to-develop-positive-respectful-communication-at-work/

WellRight. (2022, March 15). *Getting past the top 5 barriers to DEI program implementation.* Wellright. https://www.wellright.com/blog/getting-past-top-5-barriers-dei-program-implementation

Williams, J. C., & Dolkas, J. (2022, March 1). *Data-driven diversity.* Harvard Business Review. https://hbr.org/2022/03/data-driven-diversity#:~:text=According%20to%20Harvard%20Kennedy%20School

Yale. (n.d.). *Learn and grow: What is adaptability in the workplace?* Your Yale. https://your.yale.edu/learn-and-grow-what-adaptability-workplace#:~:text=Practicing%20adaptability%20may%20include%20how

Zane, M. (2022, September 26). *How to show respect in the workplace.* Zippia. https://www.zippia.com/advice/respect-in-the-workplace/

www.ingramcontent.com/pod-product-compliance
Lightning Source LLC
Chambersburg PA
CBHW071211210326
41597CB00016B/1771